THE ACTS OF THE APOSTLES

NEW TESTAMENT FOR SPIRITUAL READING

VOLUME 11

Edited by

John L. McKenzie, S.J.

THE ACTS
OF THE APOSTLES

Volume 2

JOSEF KÜRZINGER

CROSSROAD · NEW YORK

1981
The Crossroad Publishing Company
575 Lexington Avenue, New York, NY 10022

Originally published as *Die Apostelgeschichte 2*
© 1970 by Patmos-Verlag
from the series *Geistliche Schriftlesung*
edited by Wolfgang Trilling
with Karl Hermann Schelke and Heinz Schürmann

English translation © 1971 by Sheed and Ward, Ltd.
Translated by Simon and Erika Young

Library of Congress Catalog Card Number: 81-68167
ISBN: 0-8245-0120-9

OUTLINE

THE WORK OF THE APOSTLE TO THE GENTILES: FROM ANTIOCH TO ROME
(13:1—28:32)

Barnabas and Saul, Paul: their missionary journey through Cyprus and Asia Minor (13:1—14:28)

Ceremonial Sending-Off from Antioch (13:1-3)

¹*Now in the church at Antioch there were prophets and teachers, Barnabas, Symeon who was called Niger, Lucius of Cyrene, Manaen a member of the court of Herod the tetrarch, and Saul. ²While they were worshipping the Lord and fasting, the Holy Spirit said, " Set apart for me Barnabas and Saul for the work to which I have called them." ³Then after fasting and praying they laid their hands on them and sent them off.*

When Luke, whom we regard as the author of Acts, wants to start a new section of his book, he begins by listing the names of those who will play a significant part in it. Thus at the beginning of Acts (1:13 and 26), he gives the names of the Twelve—the men who are most closely linked with the formation of the original community at Jerusalem. When he goes on to describe the further development of the Church, he introduces us (in 6:5) to the Seven who are coopted to stimulate her internal and external growth. And now, at the beginning of the description of the Church's world-wide mission, he lists a further five names— men who will play a vital part in the highly decisive epoch of the Church's history which is now beginning.

I

Again we observe how Luke makes a point of picking out two from among those he has named, who will play the chief part in the story he is about to unfold. Among the Twelve it was Peter and John who stood out; among the Seven it was Stephen and Philip. And now, among the Five named here, it is once again two—Barnabas and Saul—on whom our attention will be fixed.

The other three, of whom we know nothing further, retire into the background, seemingly disregarded. But only " seemingly." For the very fact of their mention, and of their description as "prophets and teachers," shows that there already existed a fundamental structure in the Church. The Church, the subject matter of Acts, is not merely a spiritual or religious movement, not merely an invisible kingdom. With all its concentration on the spiritual, it is also a visible structure, tied to particular human beings who have a special responsibility for its continuing existence. Looked at in this way, " Symeon who was called Niger, Lucius of Cyrene, Manaen " and with them the entire community at Antioch can be seen to be closely involved with the story that will be recounted here.

A brief word about the community at Antioch. According to early tradition, Antioch was the birthplace of Luke. And this would explain the interest taken in the town by Acts. Antioch saw the founding of the first Gentile Christian community, whose beginnings are described in chapter 11 verses 19–30. Barnabas, the Greek-speaking Jewish Christian who was a native of Cyprus (4:36), is sent from Jerusalem to Antioch in order to look after the infant community there. From Tarsus he fetches Saul who had been more or less neglected up to that moment, and has him share in the work at Antioch. Once before already, as Paul stood for the first time in front of the Christian community at Jerusalem after the vision at Damascus, it was this same Barnabas who, according to 9:27ff., overcame their distrust of their erstwhile persecutor and enabled him to be received among them as one of the brethren.

Antioch becomes the most important starting-point for the mission to the Gentiles. Barnabas and Saul are sent out from there. They, and in particular Saul/Paul, return again and again. It is there that Paul gives an account of his work and experiences (14:26; 18:22). And it is in Antioch, in the encounter between Gentile and Jewish Christians, that there arises quite spontaneously between them that passionate quarrel in which the Jewish Christians, constricted by narrow orthodoxy and arid tradition, rise up against the Gentiles who were not bound by the law.

Thus, as the early Church develops, Antioch comes to hold a special position within her, and to enter into a state of unmistakable through fruitful tension with Jerusalem and the original community there. Soon of course Rome, the capital of the Roman Empire, whose special function it was to keep the memory of Peter and Paul alive, will replace Antioch in the public mind. And as history develops, Byzantium too will become a special focal point and enter into competition with Rome. But throughout all the ages, despite the external divisions of Christendom and the transference of administrative power, it is Jerusalem that will be honored by all who believe in Christ Jesus, as the holy city in which his Church began.

Barnabas and Saul are thereupon given special directions for the work to which the Spirit has "called" them. Does this refer to an earlier explicit call? Or is this their first intimation of God's eternal will for them? We are reminded here of Paul's words in the letter to the Galatians (1:15) in which he refers to his experience at Damascus: "But when he who had set me apart before I was born, and had called me through his grace, was pleased to reveal his Son to me, in order that I might preach him among the Gentiles, I did not confer with flesh and blood . . ."

Thus the laying on of hands has its own special significance. Even if it cannot be unambiguously inserted into our own legalistic, dogmatic series of beliefs, we must not overlook the fact that for the community who were " fasting and praying," this laying on of hands, presumably by the " prophets and teachers," must have meant more than merely a gesture of farewell. We have reason to believe that it signified a formal handing over of ecclesiastical office, and was at the same time an effective sign of the bestowal of the gifts of the Spirit that were to accompany this office.

In Cyprus (13:4-12)

*So, being sent out by the Holy Spirit, they went down to Seleucia; and from there they sailed to Cyprus. *When they arrived at Salamis, they proclaimed the word of God in the synagogues of the Jews. And they had John to assist them. *When they had gone through the whole island as far as Paphos, they came upon a certain magician, a Jewish false prophet, named Bar-Jesus. *He was with the proconsul, Sergius Paulus, a man of intelligence, who summoned Barnabas and Saul and sought to hear the word of God. *But Elymas the magician (for that is the meaning of his name) withstood them, seeking to turn away the proconsul from the faith. *But Saul, who is also called Paul, filled with the Holy Spirit, looked intently at him* ¹⁰and said, " You son of the devil, you enemy of all righteousness, full of all deceit and villainy, will you not stop making crooked the straight paths of the Lord? ¹¹And now, behold, the hand of the Lord is upon you, and you shall be blind and unable to see the sun for a time." Immediately mist and darkness fell upon him*

and he went about seeking people to lead him by the hand.
¹²Then the proconsul believed, when he saw what had occurred,
for he was astonished at the teaching of the Lord.

Luke is very aware of external events. Among the writers of the
Gospels—and Acts are a kind of gospel—he is the one most
interested in and conscious of historical interconnections. His
account in this third section of Acts leans heavily on accurate
information and knowledge of the secular world through which
the Apostles are moving in their missionary work. Thus his
geographical notes enable us to trace very exactly Paul's itinerary
through the Mediterranean, and the history and missionary
activity of the Church are shown to have a profound relationship
to contemporary historical events.

Cyprus, the birth-place of Barnabas (4:36), is the Apostles'
next goal. Barnabas is still the leader, his name is still put first.
But this will soon change as Saul is increasingly given pride of
place. Barnabas, the selfless friend, who smoothed Saul's way
into the Church he had once persecuted, now sees that same Saul
move far beyond him until he finally goes his own way, by his
own choice, as we are told in 15:36–40. Personal merit and
superior position must not stand in the way when the Spirit
of the Lord chooses a man for a special task.

The Jewish synagogues, which existed at that time in all the
larger towns of the Mediterranean, offered in Cyprus as elsewhere a ready-made opportunity for those who came to preach
the gospel of salvation. The primitive Church always went to
the synagogue first, and this included Paul, although he knew
himself to be the Apostle to the Gentiles.

The "magician" who was with the Roman proconsul
Sergius Paulus is a figure well known to the syncretism of that
time, consisting as it did of a mixture of Oriental, Jewish and
Hellenistic religions and cults. We are reminded here of the

magician Simon whom Peter met in Samaria (8:9ff.). The description "false prophet" tells us that Bar-Jesus taught a secret doctrine of his own and wished to make himself credible by making himself conspicuous. The message of the gospel stands and has always everywhere stood in direct contrast to such occurrences.

We note that it is in verse 9 of chapter 13 that the change from Saul to Paul occurs. From now on, only the name Paul is used, with the exception of the passages in 22:7-13 and 26:14 which refer back to the vision in Damascus. Why this change should be made precisely here is not certain. It would not be right to assume that it was only at this point that Paul took on his new name possibly in imitation of the proconsul Sergius Paulus. Nor can it be said that it was baptism and conversion that changed Saul into Paul. For in that case the change of name should have occurred already in chapter 9. But in fact the name Saul is still found in the passages following the account of his conversion, up to 13:9. One must take as one's starting point that this man from Tarsus, a Roman citizen from birth (16:37; 22:28), had from the beginning two names. One of these, Saul (9:4; 22:7. 13; 26:14), refers to his Jewish origin within the tribe of Benjamin (Phil. 3:5). The other, Paul, which is used in his various letters, belongs to his Roman and Greek cultural environment. There are many such examples of double names in Judaism. We are reminded of John Mark (12:25) and Jesus Justus (Col. 4:11).

We can only hazard a guess as to why the name change occurs precisely in 13:9. Here in Cyprus, and especially vis-à-vis the Roman proconsul, Paul stands for the first time in an official confrontation with the Roman-Hellenistic world. Thus it might seem appropriate to Acts to use only the name under which he was universally known in the primitive Church. Added to this is the fact that two separate traditions meet at this point, so that 13:9 can be regarded as the confluence of these traditions.

The punishment inflicted upon the magician by Paul, acting in full consciousness of his apostolic mission and of the presence of the Holy Spirit, becomes a sign of the Lord's victorious power. This blinded magician, who in his lack of vision looks for a hand to guide him, is a symbol of the darkness into which a man is plunged who rejects the offer of salvation and prevents others from seeing where salvation lies. In contrast to the magician stands the figure of the proconsul Sergius Paulus who finds faith and salvation through this same miracle, thereby making plain one of the basic elements in Acts—the importance to salvation of signs and wonders. This not only corresponds to the statements and descriptions of miracles in the Gospels, but also that the constant witness of the letters of Paul (Rom. 15:19; 1 Cor. 2:5; Gal. 3:5f.; 1 Thess. 1:5, etc.). We are reminded, moreover, of the importance of the charismatic gifts of the Spirit, as described in 1 Cor. 12-14.

In Pisidia (13:13-52)

PAUL PREACHES AT ANTIOCH (13:13-41)

[13]*Now Paul and his company set sail from Paphos, and came to Perga in Pamphylia. And John left them and returned to Jerusalem;* [14]*but they passed on from Perga and came to Antioch of Pisidia. And on the sabbath day they went into the synagogue and sat down.* [15]*After the reading of the law and the prophets, the rulers of the synagogue sent to them, saying, " Brethren, if you have any word of exhortation for the people, say it."* [16a]*So Paul stood up, and motioning with his hands said :*

Apart from the encounter with Sergius Paulus, little is said about the Apostles' missionary activity at Cyprus. The interest centers on the mainland of Asia Minor. Is it Paul who is impatient to move on? We note that now there are references to "Paul and his company." Paul moves more and more into the foreground and into the position of leader. John Mark, who is referred to in 13:5 as the assistant of Barnabas and Saul, presumably disagreed with the change in their itinerary. He leaves them when they reach the mainland. Was this due to his kinship with his cousin Barnabas (Col. 4:10)? For it was the latter who wanted to bring the message of salvation first of all to his native island of Cyprus. We are not certain of the actual reasons which impelled John Mark to leave them and return to Jerusalem. It must have been a very galling and painful decision for Paul. We know this because, according to 15:37ff., Paul refused to take John Mark with him a second time. He explicitly gave as the reason the latter's behavior at Pamphylia. Paul took John Mark's departure so seriously that he was even willing to put up with the separation from, and disagreement with, Barnabas which resulted from it.

Thus in these few indications we can already see the human element at work in the primitive Church. Different tastes and temperaments give rise to tensions and irritabilities. There is no point in a too hasty judgment as to the exact measure of fault and guilt. It could not have been easy always to accommodate oneself to a man like Paul. Acts and his own letters show him to have been hasty and tempestuous, totally convinced of the rightness of his own decisions and vehement in his dealings with others. He was a man full of tensions and contradictions who could only be subdued by him who said: "It hurt you to kick against the goads" (26:14). We can sympathize with young John Mark for preferring to go his own way. But we are told in the subsequent letter to the

Colossians (4:10) that the quarrel was healed, for " Mark the cousin of Barnabas " was with Paul when the latter was in prison.

Paul takes part in the worship of the synagogue and listens to the " reading of the law and the prophets " which he knows so well. These readings were called " Parashah " or " Haphtarah," and were intended for Jewish listeners. But Paul listened to them with the ears of a Christian, recognizing what in them was only provisional and still unfulfilled. He saw and felt what he described so movingly in 2 Cor. 3:6ff.: " Our sufficiency is from God, who has qualified us to be ministers of a new convenant, not in a written code but in the Spirit: for the written code kills, but the Spirit gives life. Now if the dispensation of death, carved in letters on stone, came with such splendor that the Israelites could not look at Moses' face because of its brightness, fading as this was, will not the dispensation of the Spirit be attended with greater splendor? . . . Indeed, in this case, what once had splendor has come to have no splendor at all, because of the splendor that surpasses it . . . Yes, to this day whenever Moses is read a veil lies over their minds; but when a man turns to the Lord the veil is removed (cf. Ex. 34:34)."

Thoughts like these would have been passing through Paul's mind as he listened to the words read in the synagogue—to all appearances like any other of the assembled Jews, but in reality so changed by his experience of Christ and of salvation that he was completely different. And we can understand how he at once accepted the invitation of the rulers of the synagogue, given to both newcomers, to address a " word of exhortation " to the assembly. Among them were born Jews, " men of Israel," and also certain Gentiles who feared God and were sympathetic to the Jewish religion. Some of these had even become full proselytes and members of the synagogue. This last group is of particular importance for it is a visible example of the Gentile hope of salvation and points to the new and greatly enlarged field of work now opening up before the Apostle.

16b" Men of Israel, and you that fear God, listen. 17The God of this people Israel chose our fathers and made the people great during their stay in the land of Egypt, and with uplifted arm he led them out of it. 18And for about forty years he bore with them in the wilderness. 19And when he had destroyed seven nations in the land of Canaan, he gave them their land as an inheritance, for about four hundred and fifty years. 20And after that he gave them judges until Samuel the prophet. 21Then they asked for a king; and God gave them Saul the son of Kish, a man of the tribe of Benjamin, for forty years. 22And when he had removed him, he raised up David to be their King; of whom he testified and said, ' I have found in David the son of Jesse a man after my heart, who will do all my will' [Ps. 89:20; 1 Sam. 13.14]. 23Of this man's posterity God has brought to Israel a Saviour, Jesus, as he promised. 24Before his coming John had preached a baptism of repentance to all the people of Israel. 25And as John was finishing his course, he said, ' What do you suppose that I am? I am not he. No, but after me one is coming, the sandals of whose feet I am not worthy to untie' [cf. Lk. 3:16].

In Peter's sermon to the Jews at Pentecost (2:14–36), we were able to see the way in which he addressed his own people. And now, in a deliberate parallel, we can see Paul doing like-wise. Later (in 14:15–17 and especially in 17:22–31) we shall see how Paul speaks to non-Jews, and once again this will be the counterpart to Peter's own address to the Gentiles (in 10:34–43). In these speeches we are able to observe yet again

how Acts and the infant Church as a whole try to give equal
weight to the utterances of Peter and Paul and to pay them
both equal attention. Though totally dissimilar in temperament
and achievements, Peter and Paul thus become linked in the
eyes of the Church as the twin " princes " of the Apostles.

If we compare Paul's address in the synagogue at Antioch
with Peter's sermon at Pentecost referred to above, and also
with certain sections of Stephen's speech to the high priest and
the council (7 : 2–53), it becomes clear how much all these
accounts owe to Luke's literary style. It is also true, of course,
that each of these speeches has its own special angle of approach,
depending on the particular situation in which it was given.

In a brief review of God's saving acts towards his " chosen "
people whom he rescued from their enslavement in Egypt,
Paul shows how the path of salvation led directly to the true
Saviour, to Jesus. The pre-Christian era is distinguished by its
provisional and temporary nature. Paul deliberately picks out
the figure of David as a reminder to his Jewish hearers of the
promise of salvation. But above all he shows how " the God of
this people Israel " reveals himself as the one who guides the
course of history in the face of all human imperfections into
the fullness of time, the coming of this Saviour. Paul deliberately
begins by placing himself within the context of the salvation
history which he shares with his Jewish hearers. But now he
moves on from his joint past with them and seeks to draw their
attention to what he will tell them about this Saviour Jesus who
has fulfilled what God has promised. The provisional aspects of
the past as compared to the fullness of time are made clear
by Jesus' forerunner, John the Baptist.

[26]" *Brethren, sons of the family of Abraham, and those among
you that fear God, to us has been sent the message of this
salvation.* [27]*For those who live in Jerusalem and their rulers,*

because they did not recognize him nor understand the utterance of the prophets which are read every sabbath, fulfilled these by condemning him. [28]*Though they could charge him with nothing deserving death, yet they asked Pilate to have him killed.* [29]*And when they had fulfilled all that was written of him, they took him down from the tree, and laid him in a tomb.* [30]*But God raised him from the dead;* [31]*and for many days he appeared to those who came up with him from Galilee to Jerusalem, who are now his witnesses to the people.* [32]*And we bring you the good news that what God promised to the fathers,* [33]*this he has fulfilled to us their children by raising Jesus; as also it is written in the second psalm,*

> ' *Thou art my Son,*
> *today I have begotten thee.'*

[34]*And as for the fact that he raised him from the dead, no more to return to corruption, he spoke in this way,*

> ' *I will give you the holy and sure blessing of David.'*

[35]*Therefore he says also in another psalm,*

> ' *Thou wilt not let thy Holy One see corruption.'*

[36]*For David, after he had served the counsel of God in his own generation, fell asleep, and was laid with his fathers, and saw corruption;* [37]*but he whom God raised up saw no corruption.*

The new form of address, "brethren," brings us to the real message of salvation. The Apostle knows that he is related to his listeners as "sons of the family of Abraham." Though a Christian he nevertheless acknowledges his relationship to Abraham. We know from the letter to the Romans (4:1–25) and the letter to the Galatians (3:6–14) how much emphasis he places, in his own belief and teaching, on the place of Abraham in the history of salvation, how he considers Abraham the father of all believers and not only of the Jews. Because of this belief in Abraham's universal fatherhood, Paul is able to address as "brethren," in a new meaning of the word, those Gentiles among his listeners who "fear God."

He speaks about the "message of this salvation." The salvation he refers to is that wrought by the promised Saviour Jesus (13:23). Paul is not thinking of Israel according to the flesh, but of the Israel of salvation history, as depicted in his letters. We read in Rom. 9:6ff.: "Not all who are descended from Israel belong to Israel, and not all are children of Abraham because they are his descendants, but 'Through Isaac shall your descendants be named' (Gen. 21:12). This means that it is not the children of the flesh who are the children of God, but the children of the promise are reckoned as descendants."

When Paul says that "those who live in Jerusalem and their rulers . . . did not recognize him," he does not thereby intend to minimize or even deny the objective responsibility of the Jews for the death of Jesus. For their true guilt lies in the fact that they did not accept the "message of this salvation" and thus rejected the "Saviour" sent by God. Yet we also recall Jesus' words from the Cross as reported by Luke: "Father, forgive them; for they know not what they do" (Lk. 23:34); and of Acts 3:17, where Peter says to the Jews: "Brethren, I know that you acted in ignorance, as did also your rulers."

Nevertheless even Luke acknowledges that the Jews were guilty of the death of Jesus. But he is also concerned to show that their guilt is mysteriously linked to the fact that by their action they contributed, without knowing it, to the fulfillment of the "utterances of the prophets" in regard to the promised Saviour. Paul points to a mystery that the human mind can barely grasp when he says: "And when they had fulfilled all that was written of him . . ." Once again we are reminded of the saying at Pentecost—that Jesus was "delivered up according to the definite plan and foreknowledge of God" (2:23), and of that other saying in 3:18: "What God foretold by the mouth

of all the prophets, that this Christ should suffer, he thus fulfilled." That Jesus' sufferings had been foretold in the Scriptures was part of the earliest teaching of the Church. The
letters of Paul subsequently confirmed this teaching, especially
in the following sentence which belongs to the most primitive
tradition: "Christ died for our sins in accordance with the
scriptures " (1 Cor. 15:3).

When Luke writes that Jesus' sufferings were the fulfillment
of Scripture, he touches on a matter of deep importance to the
Church, for he thereby makes plain that Jesus' death was no
fortuitous event but was part of God's decision and will to save.
To the Jews above all, whose expectation of salvation was totally
different, Jesus' death on the Cross presented an almost
insurmountable obstacle.

The early Christian Church taught that the real meaning of
the Cross was the resurrection of the Saviour who died on the
" tree " and was laid in the tomb. And this too is what we today
believe to be the basic message of the gospel. Once again we
find Paul touching on a theme found earlier in Peter's speeches
(cf. 2:24–35; 3:15; 10:39–43). In the passage under discussion
we are told that " they took him down from the tree, and laid
him in a tomb." But we are not told, in contrast to Luke 23:50–
56, who the " they " were. This is to underline for us the fact of
the tomb, thus emphasizing the full reality of Jesus' death.

But there is added the important statement that to this Jesus
who died and was buried happened the great miracle of life.
" God raised him from the dead." This simple sentence contains
the central mystery in which every other statement about salvation finds its source and validity. It is only through the
resurrection from the dead, which is more than simply a return
to earthly life, but is proof that Jesus was taken up into the
glory of God, that the seemingly senseless and negative message
of the Cross becomes meaningful, joyful and the true bearer of

salvation. We can understand how Paul, like Peter at Pentecost, takes his time to develop his argument and to justify his central thesis. Despite the essential mystery of Jesus' resurrection, the primitive Church is deeply concerned to show its reality and credibility. It does so by means of two very different kinds of witness, as is very clearly indicated in Paul's speech.

There is good reason for relying in the first place on those " witnesses to the people " to whom the Risen Lord appeared " for many days." We need not contrast this indefinite number of days with the " forty days " that are mentioned in 1 : 3. Luke clearly did not intend to be numerically exact about the duration of the resurrection appearances, even though, in view of the feast of Pentecost mentioned in 2 : 1, these " forty days " appear to have a certain exactitude.

The reference in Psalm 16 to the resurrection is familiar to us from Peter's use of it in his speech at Pentecost. If we take as our basis the text of the Greek Old Testament, the Septuagint, which Paul used, then free exegesis, as was customary in rabbinic scriptural commentaries, renders it not impossible to take Psalm 16 : 10—translated here by " Thou wilt not let thy Holy One see corruption "—beyond its literal meaning and make it refer to Jesus' freedom from corruption and his escape from the tomb. In order to justify this interpretation Paul relies on Is. 53 : 3 translated as " I will give you the holy and sure blessings of David "—but we have to admit that its meaning is not altogether clear in our context. The two passages are linked by the word " holy "—which reminds us of texts in which Jesus is called " holy " in a pre-eminent manner (cf. Lk. 1 : 35; 4 : 34; Jn. 6 : 69; Acts 3 : 14).

[38]" *Let it be known to you therefore, brethren, that through this man forgiveness of sins is proclaimed to you,* [39]*and by him every one that believes is freed from everything from which you could*

not be freed by the law of Moses. ⁴⁰*Beware, therefore, lest there come upon you what is said in the prophets:*

⁴¹*' Behold, you scoffers, and wonder, and perish;*
for I do a deed in your days,
a deed you will never believe, if one declares it to you.' "

The Jews found Paul's words unusually challenging. They regarded his setting aside of the law as an attack on their deeply rooted theological tradition. He is clearly aware of their silent opposition. Thus it is understandable that he goes on to give a severe warning, taking a passage from the Old Testament prophets and applying it as a threat to those who contemptuously reject Christ's offer of salvation. We are reminded of the challenging words with which Stephen quite unexpectedly changed the direction of his speech to the high priest and the council and turned it into a bitter accusation (7:51ff.). The exact meaning of the " deed " or " work " mentioned by the prophet is not clear. It seems to refer to the work of converting the world—the universal mission now begun under the guidance of the Holy Spirit. This work will come as an utter surprise to the Jews, for by it the Gentiles will experience " the righteousness of God . . . *apart* from law " (Rom. 3:21). Such an interpretation, as regards the more immediate future, need not exclude the long-term view of Christ's eschatological victory at the " close of the age " (Mt. 28:20).

SUCCESS AMONG THE GENTILES; REJECTION BY THE JEWS (13:42–52)

⁴²*As they went out, the people begged that these things might be told them the next sabbath.* ⁴³*And when the meeting of the synagogue broke up, many Jews and devout converts to Judaism followed Paul and Barnabas, who spoke to them and urged them to continue in the grace of God.*

⁴⁴*The next sabbath almost the whole city gathered together to hear the word of God. ⁴⁵But when the Jews saw the multitudes, they were filled with jealousy, and contradicted what was spoken by Paul, and reviled him. ⁴⁶And Paul and Barnabas spoke out boldly, saying, " It was necessary that the word of God should be spoken first to you. Since you thrust it from you, and judge yourselves unworthy of eternal life, behold, we turn to the Gentiles. ⁴⁷For so the Lord has commanded us, saying,*

> *' I have set you to be a light for the Gentiles, that you may bring salvation to the uttermost parts of the earth.' "*

⁴⁸*And when the Gentiles heard this, they were glad and glorified the word of God; and as many as were ordained to eternal life believed. ⁴⁹And the word of the Lord spread throughout all the region. ⁵⁰But the Jews incited the devout women of high standing and the leading men of the city, and stirred up persecution against Paul and Barnabas, and drove them out of their district. ⁵¹But they shook off the dust from their feet against them, and went to Iconium. ⁵²And the disciples were filled with joy and with the Holy Spirit.*

This passage must be seen in the context of the very many intermingled themes that are the mark of the later accounts of Paul's activities. In the background lies the tension between Jews and Gentiles, a tension whose roots go far back into the Old Testament history of the Jewish people but which reached its high point after the Exile with the pharisaic rabbinic separation from the entire non-Jewish world. Judaism did indeed have a strong missionary interest but it was rooted in the narrowness of its own arid orthodoxy and arrogant intolerance.

The outbreak of hostility against Paul and Barnabas must be seen in the light of all this. Several reasons could be combined

to account for it. Among them doubtless was anger at the
astonishing success of the two men among the Gentile population. But the deepest reason lay of course in the new teaching
itself—a teaching which was directed against the Jewish law,
and was a rejection of the Mosaic regulations governing their
daily life. Among these regulations circumcision and ritual laws
held a pre-eminent place.

How do Paul and Barnabas react to this inflammatory situation? Despite open opposition, these two servants of the gospel
fully recognize the special place of the Jewish people in Old
Testament salvation history. As Peter said to the Jews in 3:26:
"God, having raised up his servant, sent him to you first," so
Paul says here: "It was necessary that the word of God should
be spoken first to you." We are reminded, too, of Romans 1:16
where Paul speaks of the gospel as "the prayer of God for
salvation to everyone who has faith, to the Jew first and also
to the Greek." Again and again we see in Acts how Paul is
pre-eminent among those who acknowledge the prior right of
the Jews in the history of salvation and how he makes every
effort to bring the message of the gospel first of all to the
synagogue. But he invariably meets the same bitter experience
that we have just been witnessing.

A special feature in the picture of Christ's Church as por-
trayed in Acts can be seen in the last sentence of the passage
under consideration: "And the disciples were filled with joy
and with the Holy Spirit." We meet this same joy again and
again as distinguishing true believers from all the rest. This
joy comes from the acceptance of the gospel and the "power of
God" (Rom. 1:16) that is in it, as well as from the personal
experience of the mystery referred to in the New Testament
as the "Holy Spirit." Without the presence of the Spirit, as
Acts makes clear, the foundation and growth of the Church in
the world of that time would have been unthinkable. The

Church is at all times dependent on the Spirit for life and the giving of life. It may be that the troubles of our time are due to the fact that we are not giving first consideration to the living power of the Spirit in the Church.

At Iconium: Success and Flight (14:1-7)

¹Now at Iconium they entered together into the Jewish synagogue, and so spoke that a great company believed, both of Jews and of Greeks. ²But the unbelieving Jews stirred up the Gentiles and poisoned their minds against the brethren. ³So they remained for a long time, speaking boldly for the Lord, who bore witness to the word of his grace, granting signs and wonders to be done by their hands.

Iconium, situated on the crowded via Sebaste, the imperial highway, had a Jewish colony, like all other important business centers. The story of Antioch of Pisidia repeats itself here. At first the Apostles' words are listened to attentively. But soon the " unbelieving " people are filled with hatred and hostility. They are called " unbelieving " because their atrophied traditions prevented them from hearing the message of salvation. Again, as at Antioch, they stir up hatred and enmity against the messengers of the gospel, who are referred to as " brethren " as a way of underlining their awareness of the tie binding together all those who believe in Christ. How often has this method of inciting hatred and discrimination appeared at least externally successful against the work of a Paul. How often in later ages has it been used by the opponents of the Christian Church.

But it cannot really succeed—and it is one of the purposes of this book to keep on saying so—where faith and trust, grace and the power of the Spirit, come to meet it face to face, freely trusting the Lord. It is the Lord who is present in the power of the Spirit (1:8) and he reveals his presence and bears "witness to the word of his grace." "Word of his grace" is a true description of the gospel.

Again we notice how greatly this first mission depended on "signs and wonders" which gave credibility to the statements of human witnesses and made it impossible for those who were genuinely seeking the truth to reject the "word." If human reason alone tries to grapple with the mystery of revelation, if men try to grasp hold of and explain revelation with the sole aid of critical and speculative thought, then there is danger that the mysteries of faith, despite all human endeavor, will come to pieces and dissolve in their hands. In this age of little faith, we have a special need for "signs" to stand in the service of our message as true witnesses to the Holy Spirit. This need for signs has nothing whatever to do with the sensation-mongers' thirst for miracles.

4But the people of the city were divided; some sided with the Jews, and some with the apostles. 5When an attempt was made by both Gentiles and Jews, with their rulers, to molest them and to stone them, 6they learned of it and fled to Lystra and Derbe, cities of Lycaonia, and to the surrounding country; 7and there they preached the gospel.

Stoning was the Jewish penalty for blasphemy. We note that the hostility of the Jews is increasing. At Antioch they were content merely with driving the Apostles out of the district. But soon it will come to an actual stoning (14:19). Here however the messengers of the gospel are able to escape from the threats of their attackers.

At Lystra (14:8–20)

A MIRACLE OF HEALING AND ITS MISINTERPRETATION BY THE GENTILES (14:8–18)

8Now at Lystra there was a man sitting, who could not use his feet; he was a cripple from birth, who had never walked. 9He listened to Paul speaking; and Paul, looking intently at him and seeing that he had faith to be made well, 10said in a loud voice, " Stand upright on your feet." And he sprang up and walked.

We are told the story of the healing of the crippled man at Lystra first and foremost because of the desire of the author of Acts to give equal and parallel importance to the work of Peter and Paul. This undeniable tendency does not mean that the accounts as such lack historical truth. But it is true that the details—for example the description of the illness, and of the behavior of the cured man—may have been influenced by the writer's desire for symmetry.

The man is healed who " had faith to be made well." The word is obviously used in its twofold meaning of bodily and spiritual health. The faith of the sick man, as the story goes, may in the first place have been directed towards the cure of his bodily sickness. But for Paul the cure belonged in the realm of salvation history. Emphasis is laid on the way the sick man " listened " to Paul. Only if we are prepared to listen to the message of salvation shall we experience within ourselves that unconditional trust in God which goes beyond mere passive, accepting faith and transcends all thought of bodily need, and ultimately makes effective the power of God's healing.

11And when the crowds saw what Paul had done, they lifted up their voices, saying in Lycaonian, " The gods have come down to us in the likeness of men!" [12]*Barnabas they called Zeus, and Paul, because he was the chief speaker, they called Hermes.* [13]*And the priest of Zeus, whose temple was in front of the city, brought oxen and garlands to the gates and wanted to offer sacrifice with the people.*

The belief that the gods are able to take on human form does, after all, reflect a serious view of the supernatural, however much it is clothed in mythological garb. It was in this same region of Lystra that there existed the charming legend of Zeus and Hermes, disguised as travelers, being welcomed by the poor couple Philemon and Baucis, whom they subsequently rewarded in a god-like manner. Behind the naïve and often child-like ideas expressed in these stories we catch glimpses of human longings for the divine.

[14]*But when the apostles Barnabas and Paul heard of it, they tore their garments and rushed out among the multitude, crying,* [15]*" Men, why are you doing this? We also are men, of like nature with you, and bring you good news, that you should turn from these vain things to a living God who made the heaven and the earth and the sea and all that is in them.* [16]*In past generations he allowed all the nations to walk in their own ways;* [17]*yet he did not leave himself without witness, for he did good and gave you from heaven rains and fruitful seasons, satisfying your hearts with food and gladness."* [18]*With these words they scarcely restrained the people from offering sacrifice to them.*

This speech excites much comment. It is in fact the first speech reported in Acts that is exclusively addressed to the Gentiles. In Paul's later speech on the Areopagus (17:23–31) we shall be shown in greater detail how he tries to explain his message to non-Jewish hearers.

Once again we have here a Pauline counterpart to the speech Peter made to the centurion Cornelius and to those who were with him (10:34–43). We note, however, that Peter speaks more precisely and fully about Jesus' saving act than does Paul. At Lystra Paul confines himself exclusively to the religious experiences of the Gentiles and in no way touches on the true message of the gospel. But we must not forget that, as we are told in 14:7 and 9, Paul had already addressed the people at Lystra on an earlier occasion, and that here his words are intended simply to correct their error as regards the messengers of the gospel.

Even so it remains highly instructive to note how the Apostles in their preaching—and in particular Paul himself—use as their starting point what is already present in the minds of their hearers. When Paul preaches to the Jews, he begins by using Old Testament statements as evidence for the truth of the gospel. But when he is preaching to the Gentiles, he tries to adapt his thought to their own preconceptions. The Christian message seeks at all times to understand the spiritual situation of the men to which it is addressed and to take this into account when formulating and setting out its explanation of its message.

SECOND PERSECUTION BY THE JEWS (14:19–20)

[19]*But Jews came there from Antioch and Iconium; and having persuaded the people, they stoned Paul and dragged him out of the city, supposing that he was dead.* [20]*But when the disciples gathered about him, he rose up and entered the city; and on the next day he went on with Barnabas to Derbe.*

Paul's letters are a clear confirmation of the people's hatred for him. In 2 Cor. 11:24 he tell us: " Five times I have received at the hands of the Jews the forty lashes less one. Three times I have been beaten with rods; once I was stoned." And in 11:26 he explicitly follows the phrase " danger from robbers " by " danger from my own people." He is referring to the same people of whom he said in Rom. 9:2f.: " I have great sorrow and unceasing anguish in my heart. For I could wish that I myself were accursed and cut off from Christ for the sake of my brethren, my kinsmen by race."

Paul, whom the crowd believed to be dead, rose up from the stones that had been thrown at him. Did he not say in 2 Cor. 4:16: " So we do not lose heart. Though our outer nature is wasting away, our inner nature is being renewed every day." And in the same letter (6:4ff.), he says: " As servants of God we commend ourselves in every way: through great endurance, in afflictions, hardships, calamities, beatings, imprisonments, tumults . . . as dying, and behold we live; as punished, and yet not killed . . .''

Paul Returns to Antioch (14:21–28)

[21]*When they had preached the gospel to that city and had made many disciples, they returned to Lystra and to Iconium and to Antioch,* [22]*strengthening the souls of the disciples, exhorting them to continue in the faith, and saying that through many tribulations we must enter the kingdom of God.* [23]*And when they had appointed elders for them in every church, with prayer and fasting, they committed them to the Lord in whom they believed.*

We are not told why the Apostles, after their success at Derbe, started on their return journey and did not, as might have been expected, continue in the direction of Paul's birth place. No doubt they wanted to revisit the churches they had already founded but had not been able fully to institute and organize on a regular basis, on account of the persecutions. Above all they needed to appoint " elders." We have no serious reason to doubt the historical accuracy of their itinerary. In the nature of the case new groups of believers needed a secure foundation and a definite organization. The Jewish-Christian church at Jerusalem had " elders " too (11:30), in imitation of Jewish communities.

We cannot be sure how far the appointment of elders was equivalent to the conferring of ecclesiastical office in the sacramental sense of Orders. Since it was accompanied by " prayer and fasting," as in 13:2 when Barnabas and Paul were sent out on their mission, we may well take it in that sense. But on the other hand the " prayer and fasting " may refer to the already existing community which was thereby committed " to the Lord." Whatever be the truth of the matter, we find in the securing and ordering of the churches the beginning of true Church organization which comes to visible expression in the appointment of elders and the tasks given to them.

[24]Then they passed through Pisidia, and came to Pamphylia. [25]And when they had spoken the word in Perga, they went down to Attalia; [26]and from there they sailed to Antioch, where they had been commended to the grace of God for the work which they had fulfilled. [27]And when they arrived, they gathered the church together and declared all that God had done with them, and how he had opened a door of faith to the Gentiles. [28]And they remained no little time with the disciples.

Even in this dry, statistical listing of facts we can discern the spirit of the gospel. Luke talks of the " grace of God," to which the messengers of salvation had been " commended " at

Antioch. The "work" which the two men had "fulfilled" was something other than the work of commerce or scholarship. The Apostles were clearly aware of this when they told the community that had sent them out "all that God had done with them, and how he had opened a door of faith to the Gentiles." This is one of the basic themes in the Book of Acts concerning the Church's growth and development.

Problems Connected with the Mission to the Gentiles: Paul and Barnabas Appear before the General Assembly of the Church in Jerusalem (15:1–35)

How These Problems Arose at Antioch (15:1–2)

¹*But some men came down from Judea and were teaching the brethren, "Unless you are circumcised according to the custom of Moses, you cannot be saved." ²And when Paul and Barnabas had no small dissension and debate with them, Paul and Barnabas and some of the others were appointed to go up to Jerusalem to the apostles and the elders about this question.*

What is said here and its continuation is of truly universal significance. If we look at the matter superficially, we may get the impression that the problem under discussion is a purely local one and does not concern us now. But a closer examination of motives and causes will make it clear that the result of the conflict will decide, for all time, the very nature and being of the Church. Looked at in this way the account in 15: 1–35 becomes, in a certain sense, the focal point of Acts, even if it does not determine the pattern of the book as a whole.

The question raised was not entirely new. Even at the time of the Gentile Cornelius' baptism, certain criticisms were being made (11:1ff.). But these referred primarily to Peter eating with the " uncircumcised." In 11:18 we saw how Peter was able to silence his critics. When the first Gentile Christian community was founded at Antioch, the question seemed to have arisen whether these Gentile Christians were obliged to observe the Jewish law. According to 11:23ff. and also Gal. 2:12, everyone appeared to accept that the new Christians concerned themselves very little with the Jewish law. Barnabas and Saul (11:25f.) seem not only to have tolerated but even encouraged this.

One may ask therefore why the conflict should suddenly have broken out with such ferocity. It may have been due to the fact that, as a result of Barnabas and Saul's successful missionary activity, Gentiles were now joining the Church in increasingly large numbers, while at the same time the pharisaically orientated group of Jewish Christians drew closer and closer together and began increasingly to see in the Gentiles' freedom from the law a betrayal of the hallowed Jewish tradition. It is easy to accuse the Jews of deliberate maliciousness. But we must not forget that they had been religiously conditioned for centuries to believe in the meticulous observance of the Mosaic law as the necessary basis for all righteousness. The difficulty of bringing an old, time-honored tradition into line with changing contemporary needs and requirements remains, after all, one of the continuing preoccupations of the Church.

Thus Barnabas and Paul's decision to go from Antioch to Jerusalem in order to make a stand of principle on freedom and the unity of the Church was of universal historical significance. That they turned to Jerusalem in the first place is a sign that they—without prejudicing their own independence—recognized the authority of the Church at Jerusalem and sought a solution in frank discussion with it. Here we meet a characteristic feature of the early Church which has remained unchanged throughout all the future crises in Church history, right up to the present day and the tensions that threaten to overwhelm us all.

Paul and Barnabas Arrive at Jerusalem (15 : 3-5)

³So, being sent on their way by the church, they passed through both Phoenicia and Samaria, reporting the conversion of the Gentiles, and they gave great joy to all the brethren. ⁴When they came to Jerusalem, they were welcomed by the church and the apostles and the elders, and they declared all that God had done with them. ⁵But some believers who belonged to the party of the Pharisees rose up, and said, " It is necessary to circumcise them, and to charge them to keep the law of Moses."

Luke is very fond of statements like the one in 15:3. Perhaps this is due to his literary style. But on the other hand we have already commented on his desire to show how those to whom the risen Lord had said " You shall be my witness in Jerusalem and in all Judea and Samaria and to the end of the earth " (1:8) were continuously " on their way," using every opportunity their travels provided to give direct or indirect witness to the onset of the kingdom. The account of the successful mission to the Gentiles, which they gave in the course of their journey, was intended to be joy-giving and to encourage in their listeners a sense of shared responsibility. Information shared among the churches is a useful way of arousing the spirit of faith and an awareness of community. A well-organized church-information service is a real missionary necessity.

Peter Clarifies (15 : 6-11)

⁶The apostles and the elders were gathered together to consider this matter. ⁷And after there had been much debate, Peter rose

and said to them, " Brethren, you know that in the early days
God made choice among you, that by my mouth the Gentiles
should hear the word of the gospel and believe. ⁸*And God who*
knows the heart bore witness to them, giving them the Holy
Spirit just as he did to us; ⁹*and he made no distinction between*
us and them, but cleansed their hearts by faith. ¹⁰*Now therefore*
why do you make trial of God by putting a yoke upon the neck
of the disciples which neither our fathers nor we have been able
to bear? ¹¹*But we believe that we shall be saved through the*
grace of the Lord Jesus, just as they will."

The demands of the Judaizers led to the official assembling of
the Jerusalem authorities. We are told of " apostles " and, as
in 15:3f., of " elders." We had already heard about the latter
in 11:30. The number of church officials had grown. Peter,
as befitted his position, gave the essence of the situation. This
is the only place in the entire third section of Acts (from
chapters 13 to 28) in which he is referred to by name. But it
is enough to indicate that nothing has changed in regard to his
office as head, and that there is no need to assume that, with
his early departure from Jerusalem (12:17), he had transferred
the leadership of the Church to James. We shall soon see, however, that James did have a special place in the church at
Jerusalem.

Peter's word referred explicitly to the case of Cornelius which
Acts makes a point of discussing at great length in 10:1—11:18.
Peter tells them that it was " God " who sent him to receive
the Roman Gentile into the Church. The sign of the " Holy
Spirit " coming upon the assembly on that occasion (10:44–48)
was the cause of Peter's decision to receive Cornelius and his
company into the community of Christ by baptism.

It might be Paul speaking. And when Peter says that God
" cleansed their hearts by faith," that is, had brought them

from sin to righteousness (cf. Rom. 3:21ff.), we have to assume that Acts uses this form of words quite deliberately. Again it sounds like Paul speaking when Peter tells them of the "yoke" of the law which not even the Jews have been able to bear. We are reminded here of Rom. 2:17–24 and of other places in the letters of Paul, and also of passages in the gospel, for example Matthew 23:4: "They bind heavy burdens, hard to bear, and lay them on men's shoulders; but they themselves will not move them with their fingers." It is these very words from the gospel which give us the basis of Peter's support for what was to become the principal theme of our text.

James Gives His Views (15:12–21)

[12]*And all the assembly kept silence; and they listened to Barnabas and Paul as they related what signs and wonders God had done through them among the Gentiles.* [13]*After they finished speaking, James replied, "Brethren, listen to me.* [14]*Symeon has related how God first visited the Gentiles, to take out of them a people for his name.* [15]*And with this the words of the prophets agree, as it is written,*

> [16]*After this I will return,*
> *and I will rebuild the dwelling of David, which has fallen;*
> *I will rebuild its ruins,*
> *and I will set it up,*
> [17]*that the rest of men may seek the Lord,*
> *and all the Gentiles who are called by my name,*
> [18]*says the Lord, who has made these things known from of old.'*

[19]*Therefore my judgment is that we should not trouble those of the Gentiles who turn to God,* [20]*but should write to them*

to abstain from pollutions of idols and from unchastity and from what is strangled and from blood. ²¹For from early generations Moses has had in every city those who preach him, for he is read every sabbath in the synagogues."

We are told in only a single sentence how Barnabas and Saul described to the assembly the mission they had just accomplished. It did not seem necessary to the writer of the Acts to go into details, especially as he had already given his readers an adequate insight into the activities of the two Apostles. Once again we note the reference to " signs and wonders."

James, referred to in Gal. 1 : 19 as " the Lord's brother," whose membership in the Twelve is in dispute, was a leading member of the community at Jerusalem. He was a Christian who was still closely bound up with the Jewish way of life, and was therefore especially valuable to the conservative elements in the Jewish Christian Church—so Gal. 2 : 12 seems to indicate—and apparently also to the extremists among the Judaizers.

Luke deliberately places James within the context of the Council of the Apostles. He quotes James' words as a way of showing the Council's attitude to the problem of the Gentile Christians and their freedom from the Jewish law. But there is no justification for concluding, simply because he had the last word in the discussion, that James spoke as the leader of the Church at Jerusalem to whom, according to 12 : 17, Peter relinquished his office. Nor would it be right to assume that he deliberately ignored Barnabas and Saul or that the words, " Brethren, listen to me," indicated that he thought of himself as one responsible, on whom the decision depended. Such a view would only be justified by the existence of a state of ill-feeling between James and Paul, with particular reference to the polemic of James' letters. But for this we have no evidence. It is true, of course, that James and Paul express themselves differently about salvation. Each lays stress on what appeals to him most. But when we look on the picture as a whole, we do not find two opposing teachings.

Nevertheless it is clear how important for this account of the first " Council " of the Church was the fact that not only Peter, but the far more traditional James, taught as a *basic principle* the freedom of the Gentiles from the law, and even called on Scripture in support. This scriptural reference, which is taken from the Greek translation of the Old Testament and freely interpreted, cannot be considered evidence in the strictest sense. It is rather an attempt to place the message to the Gentiles against the background of the prophetic expectation which saw the Israel of the future as a mighty fellowship of all those who united in seeking God.

The importance of our account lies in the fact that James shows himself to be in agreement with the basic principles of Peter—here deliberately referred to by the Hebraic form of his name, " Symeon," not the more usual " Simon." Compared to this, James' own suggestions about the fourfold prohibitions are of secondary importance. They concern precepts which, as Leviticus has it in 17:10–15 and 18:26, had already long ago been laid on strangers who lived as settlers in Israel. According to rabbinic theology, these precepts belonged to the so-called " commands of Noah " (Gen. 9:4) who had made them applicable to the whole of mankind. We have to assume that the Jews, even when in the diaspora, exacted obedience to such commands from the Gentiles whom they received among themselves as " fearing," that is, honoring God.

For Paul, (who, however, does not refer to them in Gal. 2:1–10), James' stipulations do not signify any real intervention in his own missionary work. For it is clear from 1 Cor. 8–10 that he warns Christians of the " pollutions of idols." Acts

15:29 tells us that he is thinking of " what has been sacrificed to idols." " Unchastity " seems to refer to the incestuous sexual relationships that were prohibited in Leviticus 18 : 6–18, and which, according to 1 Cor. 5, Paul also condemned. Refraining " from what is strangled and from blood " refers to the old cultic prescriptions found in Ex. 22:30; Lev. 7:24; 17:15; Deut. 14:21, according to which the tasting of blood and the eating of animals that had not been slaughtered was forbidden.

It is not clear from Paul's letters whether, and to what extent, he required from the Gentiles obedience to James' injunctions regarding the abstention from what was " strangled " and from " blood." He scarcely regarded them as strict commandments, but more as rulings for difficult situations. We remember what he said in 1 Cor. 9:20: " To the Jews I became as a Jew, in order to win Jews; to those under the law I became as one under the law—though not being myself under the law—that I might win those under the law." And Romans 14:1–23 tells us how he asked for understanding and tolerance from those who were respectively weak and strong in faith. Without denying the fourfold prohibition in James' speech, Paul was able to write as follows in a letter addressed exclusively to Gentile Christian communities: " Those, I say, who were of repute, added nothing to me " (Gal. 2:6).

That James' suggestions were not part of the law in the strict sense but were concerned with directives which would make easier the communal life of Jewish and Gentile Christians in religiously mixed areas, is shown by the explicit reference to Moses whose law was read in all the synagogues of the Jewish diaspora and thus was also known to the surrounding Gentiles.

The Assembly Decides (15 : 22–29)

²²*Then it seemed good to the apostles and the elders, with the*

whole church, to choose men from among them and send them to Antioch with Paul and Barnabas. They sent Judas called Barsabbas, and Silas, leading men among the brethren, [23]with the following letter: " The brethren, both the apostles and the elders, to the brethren who are of the Gentiles in Antioch and Syria and Cilicia, greeting. [24]Since we have heard that some persons from us have troubled you with words, unsettling your minds, although we gave them no instructions, [25]it has seemed good to us in assembly to choose men and send them to you with our beloved Barnabas and Paul, [26]men who have risked their lives for the sake of our Lord Jesus Christ. [27]We have therefore sent Judas and Silas, who themselves will tell you the same things by word of mouth. [28]For it has seemed good to the Holy Spirit and to us to lay upon you no greater burden than these necessary things : [29]that you abstain from what has been sacrificed to idols and from blood and from what is strangled and from unchastity. If you keep yourselves from these, you will do well. Farewell."

The decision of the Council is put down in writing. This is significant. The Church is a properly ordered community, an organization that uses the means and methods of human secular societies. But this does not detract in any way from the Church's true nature, which puts her on a higher plane than the merely human.

This first so-called apostolic decree has become a prototype of all future decrees and official pronouncements of the Church. The form of the decree resembles that of documents used in public life at that time. Was it Luke who gave the decree its present form? We must assume that he, the man from Antioch, would have seen the original written version.

The contents do not require lengthy explanation. The Church at Jerusalem speaks to the brethren of Antioch, Syria and

Cilicia. Antioch is named first because the mission to the Gentiles originated there. It was there, too, that the quarrel arose about the convert Gentiles' freedom from the law.

The assembly at Jerusalem clearly separates itself from the activities of the Judaizers who, acting on their own initiative and without authority from the Apostles, would have brought unrest and complications into the churches. The decision was unanimous. Are we to assume from this that the Judaizers were not present or took no part? The decision seems to have been taken only by " the apostles and the elders."

Barnabas and Paul receive honorable mention. Their work to date is not only accepted for what it is but is praised as being heroic. They are " men who have risked their lives for the sake of our Lord Jesus Christ." Of the two representatives from the Church at Jerusalem, Judas Barsabbas (clearly a brother of " Joseph called Barsabbas, who was surnamed Justus," referred to in 1:23), and Silas, the latter will be mentioned again several times as the missionary companion of Paul (cf. 15:40; 16:19, and elsewhere).

The Council's decision is attributed first and foremost to the " Holy Spirit." This sheds a fundamental light on the early Church's understanding of herself. She claims more than merely juridical authority. She lives by the mystery, the " power," of the Holy Spirit who had been promised her by the Risen Lord (1:8). Only in closest union with the Spirit, who makes present the Risen Lord, do the rulers of the Church receive their power, their authority and their effectiveness.

The decree refers explicitly to the four prohibitions laid down by James—but in a somewhat different form and sequence. They are classed as " necessary "—in other translations as " absolute." But were they really, in the strictest and most absolute sense, " necessary "? Or was it not rather a case of a provisional solution, limited in time and place? The statement

in 16:4 that, as Paul and his companions " went on their way
through the cities, they delivered to them for observance the
decisions which had been reached by the apostles and elders
who were at Jerusalem," did not refer primarily to James'
prohibitions but to the general consensus of the apostles and
elders regarding the mission to the Gentiles and their freedom
from the law. However we see from 21:25 that James, the
originator of the decree, continued to show great interest in it
and its continuing validity, even after the end of the third
missionary journey.

The Decision Is Brought to Antioch (15:30-35)

[30]*So when they were sent off, they went down to Antioch; and
having gathered the congregation together, they delivered the
letter.* [31]*And when they read it, they rejoiced at the exhortation.*
[32]*And Judas and Silas, who were themselves prophets, exhorted
the brethren with many words and strengthened them.* [33]*And
after they had spent some time, they were sent off in peace by
the brethren to those who had sent them.* ([34]*But it seemed good
to Silas to remain there.*) [35]*But Paul and Barnabas remained in
Antioch, teaching and preaching the word of the Lord, with
many others also.*

The return to Antioch was more carefree than the journey to
Jerusalem had been. The tension between the two parties in the
early Church was relaxed. The letter which Judas and Silas, the
messengers from Jerusalem, brought to the Gentile Christian
community, was proof of the brethrens' friendly attitude towards
them. We can well understand that the community " rejoiced
at the exhortation." Until the arrival of this letter, they would
have been torn by bitter strife. And we know from our own

present-day experience how oppressive and depressing are dissensions within the Church. For Paul and Barnabas too, the Council had served to affirm the principles on which they had based their mission to the Gentiles. The battle with the Judaizers, who would not be satisfied, will of course go on. But now Paul can quote the Council's decision and the authority of the Church in the face of all attacks, as he does in Gal. 2:1–10. Nevertheless his stay at Antioch does not remain undisturbed. Gal. 2:11–21 tells us the story of his confrontation with Peter.

Paul's Second Missionary Journey (15:36 — 18:23)

Paul Sets Out without Barnabas (15:36-41)

³⁶*And after some days Paul said to Barnabas, " Come, let us return and visit the brethren in every city where we proclaimed the word of the Lord, and see how they are." ³⁷And Barnabas wanted to take with them John called Mark. ³⁸But Paul thought best not to take with them one who had withdrawn from them in Pamphylia, and had not gone with them to the work. ³⁹And there arose a sharp contention, so that they separated from each other; Barnabas took Mark with him and sailed away to Cyprus, ⁴⁰but Paul chose Silas and departed, being commended by the brethren to the grace of the Lord. ⁴¹And he went through Syria and Cilicia, strengthening the churches.*

It is not a matter of theological disagreements but of temperamental ones—of different human and personal interests. At the beginning of the Church's existence, and ever since, men have had to cope with their own good and less good instincts, and this human factor affected even their apostolic work. Whom are we to blame for the dispute between two friends of long standing? Had Mark's failure, of which we were told in 13.13, really been so grave? Or was Paul too obstinate and unforgiving? Or should Barnabas have refused to take his cousin Mark (Col. 4:10) with them, on account of the great task ahead? We can do no more than ask, remembering how these situations have a habit of repeating themselves in secular history and also in the history of the Church. All who have knowledge of the experiences shared by the two men in the past find the story of their dispute practically incomprehensible. It was Barnabas who, according to 9:27, was responsible for the trust and welcome which Paul, fleeing from Damascus, received from the church at Jerusalem—at first naturally suspicious. It was Barnabas who, according to 11:25f., sought out Paul, who had been almost forgotten, in Tarsus, and took him as his companion to Antioch. It was Barnabas who went with Paul on the missionary journey to Cyprus and Asia Minor and allowed Paul increasingly to become their spokesman and leader.

Now the two friends go their separate ways, both painfully disappointed no doubt, but both called to their great vocation of preacher and teacher, and bound to follow it in the way that seemed right to them. Silas, of whom we have just heard, becomes Paul's companion in place of Barnabas, and soon young Timothy will take the place of John Mark. And again—despite all human failure and personal disagreement—the message of salvation continues on its way, carried by messengers who, in Paul's words, are " men of like nature " with himself (14:15).

Through Asia Minor (16:1–8)

¹*And he came also to Derbe and to Lystra. A disciple was there, named Timothy, the son of a Jewish woman who was a believer; but his father was a Greek. ²He was well spoken of by the brethren*

*at Lystra and Iconium. ³Paul wanted Timothy to accompany him;
and he took him and circumcised him because of the Jews that
were in those places, for they all knew that his father was a
Greek. ⁴As they went on their way through the cities, they
delivered to them for observance the decisions which had been
reached by the apostles and elders who were at Jerusalem. ⁵So the
churches were strengthened in the faith, and they increased in
numbers daily.*

*⁶And they went through the region of Phrygia and Galatia,
having been forbidden by the Holy Spirit to speak the word in
Asia. ⁷And when they had come opposite Mysia, they attempted
to go into Bithynia, but the Spirit of Jesus did not allow them;
⁸so, passing by Mysia, they went down to Troas.*

Again we have one of those brief passages which, in a few con-
cise words, covers a large section of Paul's journey. It is the habit
of Acts to describe individual events in detail and then to join
these to each other by means of tightly compressed summaries.
Paul's pastoral conscientiousness does not allow him to leave
the churches he has founded to their own devices. He continues
to look after their welfare by personal visits or by written
communications.

One incident stands out—the choice of Timothy as his missionary companion. This young man, together with his mother,
had presumably become a Christian during Paul's first stay
at Lystra. 2 Tim. 1 : 5 tells us that his mother was called Eunice,
and his grandmother Lois. We have no real reason to doubt the
correctness of these names, though there is serious reason
to doubt Paul's authorship of the pastoral letters. According to
Jewish law the son of a Jewish mother was accounted a Jew.
Up to the time under discussion, Timothy had been uncircumcised. The problems of mixed marriages have always existed.
Paul wanted to take as his companion this young man who **was**

highly spoken of by all. We do not know what other, more personal, reasons there may have been for his choice. In any event, Acts and Paul's letters show us that he had chosen well. Timothy becomes a loyal and responsible co-worker in his missionary work. It often happens that the choice by an experienced member of the hierarchy of a particular young man for ecclesiastical office thereupon puts that man on the way to his future career.

The circumcision of Timothy by Paul has excited much speculation. If we remember Paul's attitude at the Council of the Apostles, described in the previous chapter, towards those who demanded circumcision as an absolute condition for salvation (15:1), and if we read the far sharper and dogmatic sounding statements in Gal. 2:1–10 and 5:2, we shall have good reason for asking why the Apostle decided, after all, to follow this traditional Jewish custom here. We remember, moreover, how forcefully and successfully he strove against the circumcision of Titus (see Gal. 2:3). How can we explain Paul's attitude? It is the result of a genuine pastoral and missionary concern. At the Council of the Apostles it was a question of a clear theological principle, concerning the mission to the Gentiles. Titus was a Gentile Christian (Gal. 2:3), Timothy was accounted a Jew. The Jews in Lystra violently opposed Paul and his work. This we learn from 14:19f. Paul will not have forgotten how he lay half dead in Lystra beneath the stones thrown at him by his enemies. Thus he makes a compromise but not one that contradicts his strict principles as regards the Gentiles. We can if we like call it a pastoral tactic, but we must correctly understand his reasons for it. The Apostle was thinking of the excitable Jews of the neighborhood but also of the continuance of his work, which would continually bring him, as we shall see, into confrontation and dissension with the Jews.

On this second missionary journey Paul treads new paths. As he confesses in Rom. 15:20, it was his "ambition to preach the gospel, not where Christ has already been named." In this connection he recalls the words of the prophet: "For that which has not been told them they shall see, and that which they have not heard they shall understand" (Is. 52:15).

What we find particularly striking in this account is the twice attested fact that the "Holy Spirit" took such a concrete part in the location of their work. He forbade them "to speak the word in Asia." Was the Apostle already thinking of Ephesus, the chief city there? "The Spirit of Jesus" did not allow them "to go into Bithynia" either. We find the phrase "Spirit of Jesus" only in this part of the New Testament. In Rom. 8:9 we are told about the "Spirit of Christ." Everywhere we meet the mystery of the Spirit. From the beginning the Church is guided by this mysterious being whose power cannot be grasped by human understanding but is continually experienced in its effects. In the power of the Spirit the risen Lord who has been taken up to God remains nevertheless with his people. "I am with you always, to the close of the age," said Jesus (Mt. 28:20) when he gave his disciples their great commission to teach in his name.

In Macedonia and Greece (16:9—18:22)

HE IS CALLED TO MACEDONIA (16:9-10)

⁹*And a vision appeared to Paul in the night: a man of Macedonia and standing beseeching him and saying, "Come over to Macedonia and help us." ¹⁰And when he had seen the vision immediately we sought to go on into Macedonia, concluding that God had called us to preach the gospel to them.*

This sentence makes clear why the " Holy Spirit," the " Spirit of Jesus," has just guided the Apostle's path in such a striking manner. A great new work is opening out before them. Paul is led towards it in a dramatic way. We have no right and indeed no reason to take lightly this guidance from above, and to see it as only a literary or attention-seeking device for announcing the beginning of the mission to Europe. The description of this extraordinary missionary call by means of a vision at night of a man of Macedonia must be understood by analogy with other extraordinary happenings recounted in Acts—even though we may not be able to follow the details clearly.

It is worth noting that the passage beginning here (16: 10–17) is the first in Acts to use the pronoun " we." It may be supposed from this that it must have been transcribed from a journal of their travels kept by Luke. The " we " appears again in 20:5. Here it ends with their arrival at Philippi. And there, curiously, it begins again at Philippi; and from then on it can be traced throughout the rest of the book.

First Activities at Philippi (16:11–18)

[11]*Setting sail therefore from Troas, we made a direct voyage to Samothrace, and the following day to Neapolis,* [12]*and from there to Philippi, which is the leading city of the district of Macedonia, and a Roman colony. We remained in this city some days;* [13]*and on the sabbath day we went outside the gate to the riverside, where we supposed there was a place of prayer; and we sat down and spoke to the women who had come together.* [14]*One who heard us was a woman named Lydia, from the city of Thyatira, a seller of purple goods, who was a worshipper of God. The Lord opened her heart to give heed to what was said by Paul.* [15]*And when she was baptized, with her house-*

hold, she besought us, saying, "If you have judged me to be faithful to the Lord, come to my house and stay." And she prevailed upon us.

Paul steps onto European soil. It must have been around the year 50. The " Spirit of Jesus " had called him. Europe waits for the Gospel. It is true that there have been Christians in Italy and Rome for a considerable time, as 28 : 14f. relates; and probably also churches. These Christians seem to have been of Jewish origin. In the list of peoples in the Pentecost account (2 : 10), there is mention, and with good reason, of " visitors from Rome." Are we to assume that Peter was already in Rome before Paul's arrival in Macedonia? We do not know, but it is not impossible. We note that Paul, in his letter to the distinguished community at Rome (Rom. 15 : 23f.), does not intend to stay there for any length of time.

Thus Christianity has already taken root in one or two places. But it is only with Paul's arrival that there begins the systematic missionizing of Europe. He turns to Jews and non-Jews. The Church begins to establish itself in Europe.

Philippi becomes their first stopping place. Again Luke describes their journey with great attention to detail.

The father of Alexander the Great is commemorated in the name of the town; Caesar's murderers were finally destroyed there. The town contained a Roman colony with an autonomous administration. Perhaps it was this that moved Paul, the Roman citizen, to begin his work there. We know from the subsequent letter to the Philippians that this community always lay closer to his heart than all the other churches (Phil. 1 : 7; 4 : 15).

Again Paul turns first to the Jews. They seem to have formed a small community in a town whose inhabitants were preponderantly Roman colonists. But Paul made use of every opportunity. Only one woman let herself be baptized, together with her household. Every indication points to her not being Jewish. In Revelations 2 : 18–29 we are told about her native town, Thyatira. Lydia is one of those women found in Acts and in the letters of Paul who combined an interior readiness for the faith with the will to help personally and actively in the work. In Romans 16 Paul names these women with great respect and gratitude.

[16]*As we were going to the place of prayer, we were met by a slave girl who had a spirit of divination and brought her owners much gain by soothsaying.* [17]*She followed Paul and us, crying, " These men are servants of the Most High God, who proclaim to you the way of salvation."* [18]*And this she did for many days. But Paul was annoyed, and turned and said to the spirit, " I charge you in the name of Jesus Christ to come out of her." And it came out that very hour.*

Here we have one of those New Testament stories which depicts the world of magic and sorcery in all its dark mysterious power. We are reminded of the magician Bar-Jesus in Samaria (8 : 9ff.), and of Jesus' encounter with the possessed man who, like the slave girl in Philippi, manifested a demonic knowledge of his divine person (cf. Mk. 5 : 7).

IMPRISONMENT AND ESCAPE (16: 19–26)

[19]*But when her owners saw that their hope of gain was gone, they seized Paul and Silas and dragged them into the market place before the rulers;* [20]*and when they had brought them to the magistrates they said, " These men are Jews and they are disturbing our city.* [21]*They advocate customs which it is not lawful for us Romans to accept or practice."* [22]*The crowd joined in attacking them; and the magistrates tore the garments off them*

*and gave orders to beat them with rods. ²³And when they had in-
flicted many blows upon them, they threw them into prison,
charging the jailer to keep them safely. ²⁴Having received this
charge, he put them into the inner prison and fastened their feet
in the stocks.*

*²⁵But about midnight Paul and Silas were praying and sing-
ing hymns to God, and the prisoners were listening to them,
²⁶and suddenly there was a great earthquake, so that the foundations of the prison were shaken; and immediately all the doors
were opened and everyone's fetters were unfastened.*

The freeing of the slave girl from her demonic possession was
not looked upon kindly. The profit motive leaves no room for
higher considerations. In their anger at the material loss they
found grounds for seizing Paul and his companion. The charge
against them became a religious and political one. Their accusers spoke as " Romans " and accused Paul and Silas on the
ground that they were " Jews " whose message was disruptive
to the state. The Church and her representatives have often stood
before similar tribunals. Jesus' trial repeats itself in every age.

All this Paul had to experience at Philippi, and the curious
thing is that this time, unlike other occasions, it was not the
Jews who rose up against him but he himself and his companion
who were attacked and mishandled as " Jews." Why did not
Paul at once claim his Roman citizenship as he did on that other
occasion of his imprisonment by the Roman soldiers in Jerusalem
(22:25-29) when he thereby avoided a scourging? This is the
only time that Paul had a bad experience with the Roman
authorities, in contrast to all his other encounters with them.

The messengers of the gospel are now lying, like dangerous
criminals, in the deepest confines of the prison, their feet painfully fastened in the stocks, prevented from all movement and
unable to sleep. A scene totally in the spirit of Acts—human

weakness, helpless on the ground; and precisely at this point the indestructible power of the Lord present in his Church is revealed.

But this time too the Apostle was able to experience what later as a prisoner he was to describe in his letter to the Christians at Philippi: " It is my eager expectation and hope that I shall not be at all ashamed, but that with full courage now as always Christ will be honored in my body, whether by life or by death" (Phil. 1:20). The pressure of their bonds, the painful position in which they were tied, the burning weals on their bodies, did not prevent Paul and his companion from praying and singing to God, thus witnessing to their faith before the other prisoners. And God shows himself near. He is mightier than all human undertakings.

One may of course see in this story of Paul's liberation, which is a deliberate parallel to the liberation of Peter (12:3ff.; also 5:17ff.), echoes of other such stories in the literature of antiquity, and thus place it in the literary genre of this type. But this gives us no justification for looking on the whole picture as a merely symbolic representation whose purpose it was to show the extent to which the Apostle stood under the continuous protection of God. God shows himself effective in a very concrete manner, and his answer to the trusting prayer of his messengers is this liberation which cannot be explained by natural means.

CONVERSION OF THE JAILER (16: 27–34)

²⁷When the jailer woke and saw that the prison doors were open, he drew his sword and was about to kill himself, supposing that the prisoners had escaped. ²⁸But Paul cried with a loud voice, " Do not harm yourself, for we are all here." ²⁹And he called for lights and rushed in, and trembling with fear he fell down

*before Paul and Silas, [30]and brought them out and said, " Men,
what must I do to be saved?" [31]And they said, " Believe in the
Lord Jesus, and you will be saved, you and your household."
[32]And they spoke the word of the Lord to him and to all that
were in his house. [33]And he took them the same hour of the
night, and washed their wounds, and he was baptized at once,
with all his family. [34]Then he brought them up into his house,
and set food before them; and he rejoiced with all his household that he had believed in God.*

Behind the story of their imprisonment lies the story of their
liberation. This story is full of important themes. The Apostle,
freed by God's intervention, frees in his turn another human
being who is the prisoner of his earthly ideas. Paul saves him for
true freedom. The jailer, once the slave of his superior, then the
slave of his fear and his mistaken sense of honor, wants to kill
himself, and thereupon experiences the saving word of the
prisoner whom he had thrown into the inner prison earlier that
night. He senses the mysterious power of a higher being. The
apostles become for him the messengers of this power. The light
that he is given and with which he goes to the prisoners in the
darkness of the night becomes the symbol of a different light
which begins to shine on his path. We are reminded of the centurion Cornelius who goes to meet Peter and falls down at his
feet in expectation of salvation (10:25). The descriptions of Paul
and of Peter continually run the same course.

" What must I do to be saved?" This question in different
form runs through the whole of Acts. " What shall we do?" ask
the witnesses to the happenings at Pentecost (2:37). " What
shall I do, Lord? " asks Paul, lying on the ground, of the
Lord who had met him on his way (9:6; 22:10). " What is it,
Lord?" asks Cornelius, the centurion at Caesarea, of the angel
of God who stood before him in a vision.

The jailer asks the two Apostles: "What must I do to be saved?" Paul in his answer points to the one and only Lord: "Believe in the Lord Jesus, and you will be saved, you and your household." He is talking of the risen Lord. Salvation lies in belief in him. Belief is man's readiness for God's offer of salvation—an offer which has found its expression in Jesus' death and resurrection.

The jailer lets himself be led to belief. He and his household hear the message of salvation, the "word of the Lord," as the gospel is called here. As a sign of his faith, he shows every care for the two missionaries whom he had earlier put in the stocks, and washes the wounds they bore on their bodies from the scourging. And he lets himself be baptized, with his family. Faith and baptism belong together. They are necessary to each other. And when we are told that he set food before them, it is not difficult to believe that this food had some connection with the eucharistic breaking of bread. Again Acts speaks of the rejoicing that accompanied the encounter with the message of salvation.

EMBARRASSMENT OF THE MAGISTRATES (16:35–40)

35But when it was day, the magistrates sent the police, saying, "Let those men go." 36And the jailer reported the words to Paul, saying, "The magistrates have sent to let you go; now therefore come out and go in peace." 37But Paul said to them, "They have beaten us publicly, uncondemned, men who are Roman citizens, and have thrown us into prison; and do they now cast us out secretly? No! Let them come themselves and take us out." 38The police reported these words to the magistrates, and they were afraid when they heard that they were Roman citizens; 39so they came and apologized to them. And they took them out and asked them to leave the city. 40So they

went out of the prison, and visited Lydia; and when they had
seen the brethren, they exhorted them and departed.

The story of the foundation of the first Pauline church on European soil closes with a picture from which we can draw several
lessons. The behavior of the magistrates is surprising. What
moved them to send the unexpected message that the Apostles
were to be set free? Had they been told of the occurrence of the
previous night? It is more likely that they realized that they
had treated the two accused unjustly the day before, under
pressure from the crowd. 16:22 deliberately asserts that when
they had been brought before the magistrates, " the crowd joined
in attacking them." There is an interesting addition found in
several texts, to 16:39, where the Apostles are asked to leave the
city " so that the people will not rise up again and attack you
in our presence."

The behavior of the Apostle deserves special mention. He is
not content with a secret dismissal. He invokes his Roman
citizenship, lists the injustices done to them, and demands honorable restitution. He is not concerned with his personal honor
but with his standing as an Apostle, his calling as messenger
of the Lord. He is concerned with the Church. It is true that he
writes in 1 Cor. 6:7 that one should " suffer wrong." He says,
" Why not rather be defrauded? " And in 1 Cor. 13:7 he
writes: " Love bears all things, believes all things, hopes all
things, endures all things." In his letters he speaks again and
again of this all-forgiving love that conquers all evil. But when
it is a question of safeguarding his office and preserving his
great vocation as servant of the gospel, then he knows how to
defend himself with determination against injustice and attack.
He follows the example of Jesus who said that one should
respond to aggression by turning the other cheek, but who
nevertheless resisted every attack upon his mission and message.

Paul was successful. The magistrates came, talked to them in a friendly manner, and when they asked them to leave the city, the Apostles did so in order to avoid further unrest there. To distinguish between justified and unjustified resistance in the spirit of Christ is the gift of the Holy Spirit who guides mankind.

Paul says farewell to Lydia and the Christians who were with her. This small community is the first fruit of his European mission.

In Thessalonica (17 : 1–9)

EARLY SUCCESSES (17: 1–4)

¹Now when they had passed through Amphipolis and Apollonia, they came to Thessalonica, where there was a synagogue of the Jews. ²And Paul went in, as was his custom, and for three weeks he argued with them from the scriptures, ³explaining and proving that it was necessary for the Christ to suffer and to rise from the dead, and saying, " This Jesus, whom I proclaim to you, is the Christ." ⁴And some of them were persuaded, and joined Paul and Silas; as did a great many of the devout Greeks and not a few of the leading women.

The gospel is once again " on its way." Rejection and opposition drive it from place to place. The missionaries take the via Egnatia, the imperial highway that led from the East through Macedonia to the Adriatic. Luke carefully marks the route. They come to halt in Thessalonica. It is as though the Roman Empire had spread before them its great net of interweaving streets in order to prepare a path for their message. We know that it gave more to the gospel than simply its roads.

Paul's experience in Thessalonica was similar to what had gone before. Again he goes to the synagogue of the Jews and again he refers to the Old Testament Scriptures, in order to show them the picture of the Messiah that is to be found there. He points to the characteristics with which he is most familiar from his personal experience of Christ. In the Scriptures he finds the suffering, but also the risen Messiah. We are not given individual citations, but for these we can refer to the passages in Peter's sermons (2:23ff.; 3:18) and Paul's sermon in Antioch of Pisidia (13:27ff.), with their customary free quotations of Old Testament texts. All that the apostolic kerygma teaches us ful-filling the essential requirements of its Jewish hearers is con-tained in the solemn statement: "This Jesus, whom I proclaim to you, is the Christ."

PERSECUTION BY THE JEWS (17: 5–9)

⁵But the Jews were jealous, and taking some wicked fellows of the rabble, they gathered a crowd, set the city in an uproar, and attacked the house of Jason, seeking to bring them out to the people. ⁶And when they could not find them, they dragged Jason and some of the brethren before the city authorities, crying, " These men who have turned the world upside down have come here also, ⁷and Jason has received them; and they are all acting against the decrees of Caesar, saying that there is another king, Jesus." ⁸And the people and the city authorities were dis-turbed when they heard this. ⁹And when they had taken security from Jason and the rest, they let them go.

Again the Jews seek to thwart the mission to the Gentiles. These Jews of Thessalonica try to put their accusations onto the politi-cal plane, as the Jewish leaders had done in Jesus' trial (Lk.

23:2). This has often happened in the course of the Church's history. Again and again Christians came under the groundless suspicion of being politically unreliable.

We may feel surprise that in this case the authorities at Thessalonica contented themselves with letting Jason go surety and did not follow up so serious an accusation. Perhaps those in responsible positions recognized the true motives of the Jewish accusers, just as Pilate saw through Jesus' accusers (Mk. 15:10), and the proconsul Gallio in Corinth did not take seriously the complaints against Paul (18:14ff.).

Persecution also in Beroea (17: 10-15)

[10]*The brethren immediately sent Paul and Silas away by night to Beroea; and when they arrived they went into the Jewish synagogue.* [11]*Now these Jews were more noble than those in Thessalonica, for they received the word with all eagerness, examining the scriptures daily to see if these things were so.* [12]*Many of them therefore believed, with not a few Greek women of high standing as well as men.* [13]*But when the Jews of Thessalonica learned that the word of God was proclaimed by Paul at Beroea also, they came there too, stirring up and inciting the crowds.* [14]*Then the brethren immediately sent Paul off on his way to the sea, but Silas and Timothy remained there.* [15]*Those who conducted Paul brought him as far as Athens; and receiving a command for Silas and Timothy to come to him as soon as possible, they departed.*

Paul has to leave Thessalonica without being able to complete his work there. We read of his grief at this in the moving letter he writes to the church from Corinth. He says there: " But since we were bereft of you, brethren, for a short time, in person not in heart, we endeavored the more eagerly and with great desire to see you face to face; because we wanted to come to you—I, Paul, again and again—but Satan hindered us. For what is our hope or joy or crown of boasting before our Lord Jesus at his coming? Is it not you? For you are our glory and joy " (1 Thess. 2 : 17–20).

With sentiments like these Paul took his leave at the urging of the brethren, and sought refuge in the small town of Beroea which lay away from the main route. Here too he continues his work. The Jews of the local synagogue showed real concern for salvation and eagerly examined the meaning drawn by Paul from the Old Testament texts, and its reference to Christ Jesus. The non-Jews, who were close to the synagogue, also showed genuine interest, as did certain women of high standing whom Luke, faithful to his usual custom, does not omit to mention.

Paul was not, of course, left in peace for long. The Jews of Thessalonica, in their hatred, went after him to Boroea—a distance of 50 miles or so—just as the Jews of Antioch and Iconium had done on his first missionary journey, when they came to Lystra to persuade the people there to stone him. But this time Paul was able to escape from their threats, and was led away from the source of immediate danger, southwards towards Athens. We know how he felt about being taken away from his work from the letter he wrote to the Thessalonians: " When we could bear it no longer, we were willing to be left behind at Athens alone, and we sent Timothy, our brother and God's servant in the gospel of Christ, to establish you in your faith and to exhort you, that no one be moved by these afflictions. You yourselves know that this is to be our lot. For when we were with you, we told you beforehand that we were to suffer affliction; just as it has come to pass, and as you know. For this reason, when I could bear it no longer, I sent that I might know your faith, for fear that somehow the tempter had tempted you and that our labor would be in vain " (1 Thess. 3 : 1–5).

The story behind this sparse, condensed account is one of continuous work, worry, and the human afflictions of a man who is passionately concerned to bring God's message to men, and who could write of himself: " Woe to me if I do not preach the gospel! " (1 Cor. 9:16). Truly, this beginning of the Church on European soil was for Paul a painful round of most bitter experiences. But he knew for whom he suffered and with whom he suffered. " For the sake of Christ, then, I am content with weaknesses, insults, hardships, persecutions and calamities; for when I am weak, then I am strong " (2 Cor. 12:10).

In Athens (17: 16–34)

He Meets the Men of the City (17: 16–18)

[16]*Now while Paul was waiting for them at Athens, his spirit was provoked within him as he saw that the city was full of idols.* [17]*So he argued in the synagogue with the Jews and the devout persons, and in the market place every day with those who chanced to be there.* [18]*Some also of the Epicurean and Stoic philosophers met him. And some said, " What would this babbler say? " Others said, " He seems to be a preacher of foreign divinities "—because he preached Jesus and the resurrection.*

Again Acts makes plain how hatred and persecution open up new possibilities for the preaching of the gospel. Paul comes to Athens as a fugitive. Even though the brilliance of a Pericles, and the fame of the school of Plato had by then disappeared from that city, it was still considered a center of cultural wealth and intellectual greatness. The numerous statues point to the religious searching and longing of the people there, even though their ideas and aims might differ widely.

Paul comes with the message of the gospel. It was a momentous encounter. It is true that even here, in Athens, there is mention of the Jewish synagogue to which the Apostle, faithful to his deepest obligations, addresses himself first. But it is clear that his true interest in this city belongs to the non-Jewish, Greek world. Paul shows us here how the gospel is for all men, irrespective of the spiritual, cultural and social situation in which they may be placed, and not only for a narrowly circumscribed group.

He is not one to wait for men to come to him with their problems and longings. He goes out to the busy world of the market place where it was less a question of the exchange of goods and more of the exchange of ideas about politics, philosophy, and life. Rhetoric and sophistry still determined the intellectual life of Athens. Paul sought to enter into conversation with Epicureans and Stoics—adherents of two very different philosophies. The Epicureans concentrated on this life, and on delicacy of worldly perception. They showed little interest in God or gods. They sought happiness and peace of mind by living in accordance with a naturalistic view of the world. The Stoics represented those who tried to form their life according to their philosophy and live it according to its nature, who subjugated human drives and instincts to reason, and saw in God the immanent being in whom all things running their predetermined course were present in their essence.

Was it not a hopeless undertaking to bring the message of Jesus and his resurrection to men such as these? Would not the saving message of salvation bounce off, like drops of water on the marble of a pagan temple, before this view of the world and this philosophy of life? The situation described in our text is given credibility when we read that some of his audience in their complacent arrogance, called Paul a " babbler " while others—presumably the Stoics—held back sceptically. Paul remembers the distress he felt at his treatment in the market place at Athens in 1 Cor. 1 : 20ff. : " Where is the wise man ? Where is the scribe? Where is the debater of this age? Has not God made foolish the wisdom of the world? For since, in the wisdom of God, the world did not know God through wisdom, it pleased God through the folly of what we preach to save those who believe. For Jews demand signs and Greeks seek wisdom, but we preach Christ crucified, a stumbling block to Jews and folly to Gentiles, but to those who are called, both Jews and Greeks, Christ the power of God and the wisdom of God."

BEFORE THE AREOPAGUS (17: 19–34)

[19]*And they took hold of him and brought him to the Areopagus, saying, " May we know what this new teaching is which you present? [20]For you bring some strange things to our ears; we wish to know therefore what these things mean." [21]Now all the Athenians and the foreigners who lived there spent their time in nothing except telling or hearing something new.*

Paul is brought to the Areopagus. It is scarcely a police measure but an attempt to find out, away from the noise of the market place, what this " preacher of foreign divinities " had to say. Luke has good reason to stress the word Areopagus. At one time this word referred to the famous meeting place on the hill of " Ares." But later, it came to be more and more associated with the judicial power of the official authority which concerned itself, among other things, with the supervision of public speeches. If here we take the second meaning, Paul's situation seems indeed remarkable. The messenger of the gospel is given the possibility of delivering his message within the official framework of the representatives of Greek culture.

This man from Tarsus has " strange things " to tell them. Was their interest genuine? The reference to the Athenians' love of " telling or hearing something new " does not point to true readiness for salvation. The love of gossip which we find among the Athenians is universal. People speak and write about religion and eagerly take part in intellectual discussion of theological questions, but do not show a true desire for personal commitment and response to the truth.

[22]*So Paul, standing in the middle of the Areopagus, said: " Men of Athens, I perceive that in every way you are very religious.* [23]*For as I passed along, and observed the objects of your worship, I found also an altar with this inscription: ' To an unknown god.' What therefore you worship as unknown, this I proclaim to you.* [24]*The God who made the world and everything in it, being Lord of heaven and earth, does not live in shrines made by man,* [25]*nor is he served by human hands, as though he needed anything, since he himself gives to all men life and breath and everything.* [26]*And he made from one every nation of men to live on all the face of the earth, having determined allotted periods and the boundaries of their habitation,* [27]*that they should seek God, in the hope that they might feel after him and find him. Yet he is not far from each one of us,* [28]*for*

' In him we live and move and have our being ';
as even some of your poets have said,
' For we are indeed his offspring.'

[29]*Being then God's offspring, we ought not to think that the Deity is like gold, or silver, or stone, a representation by the art and imagination of man.* [30]*The times of ignorance God overlooked, but now he commands all men everywhere to repent,* [31]*because he has fixed a day on which he will judge the world in righteousness by a man whom he has appointed, and of this he has given assurance to all men by raising him from the dead."*

The speech on the Areopagus in the form in which we have it is a literary masterpiece which tellingly describes Paul's actual situation. Already in Lystra (14:14ff.) the Apostle had endeavored to adapt his speech to the religious experience and ideas of his listeners. And he does this in even stronger measure here. As has already been said, this speech of Paul's to his non-Jewish hearers is shown in Acts as a parallel to Peter's speech to the centurion Cornelius and his circle. The speech on the Areopagus, however, is more profoundly orientated towards the minds of its listeners than was Peter's speech. What we miss in the speech on the Areopagus are the really "Christian" elements, but this is so because Paul was not allowed to finish in the sense we expect. He intended to link the true message of salvation to his words about Jesus' resurrection. For this reason also there is no mention of the word "faith" which belongs to the essence of the Pauline and indeed of the whole New Testament message.

Paul begins his speech with the classical form of address, "Men of Athens." And though, as we read in 17:16, his "spirit was provoked" within him as he saw that the city was full of idols, he nevertheless manages to find appreciative words when he says, "I perceive that in every way you are very religious." This is a psychologically effective attempt at making contact. Paul does not all at once overwhelm his listeners with the fullness of the message he has to bring them. He begins by directing their attention to the knowledge of God. Only the man who is led to know God will be ready to hear the message contained in the gospel. It was an exceptionally effective way for Paul to begin his speech by pointing to the altar of an unknown God as a way of referring to the Athenians' unfulfilled searching and longing. We do not know what was in the mind of the man who gave the altar the inscription—"To an unknown God." Was he motivated by the fear of overlooking any one of the many gods? Or is the inscription the expression of the awe man feels before the mysterious world of gods and the

divine? We must not forget that already long before Paul Greek
men of learning had striven towards a noble concept and defini-
tion of God.

Paul points to the inscription about the one God whom he
knows from the Bible and still more as a Christian from his
encounter with the risen Christ. He does not speak with the
learning of philosophers, but as a preacher and witness. And yet
he takes account of the intellectual habits of his listeners when
he goes on to speak of the transcendent glory of this all-powerful
creator God, who is not to be found within the narrow confines
of temples and images and who, himself in need of nothing,
opens himself out to the neediness of man.

When Paul says that this God gives to all men " life and
breath and everything " that they need, we are reminded of the
creation story in the Bible where it is said (Gen. 2 : 7) that " the
Lord God formed man of dust from the ground, and breathed
into his nostrils the breath of life." But it is also possible that
Acts wants to make a play of words with the name " Zeus,"
which was traditionally associated with the Greek word for
" living " (zaein). In a hymn to Zeus, he was lauded as the
" living one " and the " breath of all creatures."

Thus Hellenistic thoughts and ideas are brought into a living
encounter with the message of the Bible. But the Bible always
leads the way, though unobtrusively. This is true, too, of the
statement concerning man's origin " from one," which refers to
Adam, the father of the human race, and for the statement about
the history of man in the world which is guided by God who
has " determined allotted periods and the boundaries of their
habitation." A reference to Luke 21 : 35 makes clear how much
of this phraseology is due to him. There, in an echo of Isaiah
24 : 17, the human race is described as " all who dwell upon the
face of the whole earth."

The Apostle's speech becomes more and more compelling, as

he talks about the special duty of men who were created by God to "seek God, in the hope that they might feel after him and find him." Here Paul touches on the deepest meaning of human life. He refers directly to the numerous attempts made by the Greeks to come to the knowledge and experience of God, whether by rational or mystical means. The essence of the Apostle's thought here already contains, of course, the seed of his message of salvation. But still he holds back and seeks to adapt himself to the ideas of his hearers.

" The times of ignorance " is what the Apostle, in a surprisingly harsh judgment, calls the age of paganism that has existed up to now. Even though he is aware that this paganism had its moments of recognition and illumination, he nevertheless sees in the widespread and multifarious worship of idols only error and ignorance. He gives a moving and vivid description of this in his letter to the Romans (1:18–32) when he depicted the customs of the non-Jewish world.

In that letter he sets against the dark picture of an ignorant, sinful humanity the joyful news of the coming of salvation (Rom. 3:21ff.). And so too he does here, in Athens. He speaks of God's command to " all men everywhere to repent." He mentions no name as yet, but speaks of " a man " whom God has appointed to " judge the world in righteousness." We know of whom he is speaking. And only now, that he has caught and held their attention, does he go on to the message of salvation and begin to speak of him whom God " has appointed. And of this," he goes on, "'he has given assurance to all men by raising him from the dead." Again, as always in his preaching and his letters, he points to the sign of Jesus' resurrection as the foundation of salvation and saving faith. And his address is so formulated that only now will he lay before them the fullness of the message. But he is not able to complete it, for his listeners are not prepared to listen any longer.

²²Now when they heard of the resurrection of the dead, some mocked; but others said, " We will hear you again about this." ²³So Paul went out from among them. ³⁴But some men joined him and believed, among them Dionysius the Areopagite and a woman named Damaris and others with them.

Where men are impelled by mere greed for knowledge and love of sensation, they will not easily find true faith. Did not Jesus himself in his stirring Messianic cry (see Mt. 11 : 25ff.) speak in the same way? " I thank thee, Father, Lord of heaven and earth, that thou hast hidden these things from the wise and understanding and revealed them to babes; yea, Father, for such was thy gracious will. All things have been delivered to me by my Father; and no one knows the Son except the Father, and no one knows the Father except the Son and any one to whom the Son chooses to reveal him."

Why do the holy texts seem to dissolve in our hands so that they no longer lead us to the mystery of God which, ultimately, opens itself only to those who come in reverent faith? We do not wish to decry men's efforts to come to a rational and reasonable understanding of what is said in the gospel. But it can easily happen that we find ourselves confronted by a plenitude of interpretations which, in their often contradictory variety, block our path to true belief.

At Corinth (*18 :1–22*)

WITH AQUILA AND PRISCILLA (18:1–3)

¹After this he left Athens and went to Corinth. ²And he found a Jew named Aquila, a native of Pontus, lately come from Italy with his wife Priscilla, because Claudius had commanded all the

*Jews to leave Rome. And he went to see them; ³and because he
was of the same trade he stayed with them, and they worked,
for by trade they were tentmakers.*

Corinth was a very different city from Athens. It had been re-
built after 46 B.C., and thanks to its position had become a trad-
ing center between East and West. It was the capital of the
Roman province of Achaia, the seat of the proconsul, and was
filled with people from every nation—people who were driven
to the city by the desire for work and money, love of the gay
life and material pleasures. If one reads the letters Paul wrote to
the Corinthian community after his first mission to them, one
will see from his admonitions and anxious care for them how
lively and restless these people of Corinth were, but also how
ready for the gospel.

Two fugitives meet together. Paul, who fled from the spiritual
blindness of the intellectually arrogant Athenians, meets the
Jews Aquila and Priscilla, who had been driven out of Rome.
Aquila's wife is here called Priscilla, but in Paul's letters (Rom.
16: 3; 1 Cor. 16: 19; 2 Tim. 4: 19) she is Prisca. We must assume
this husband and wife were already Christian, for they had been
driven from Rome by the Emperor Claudius' edict against the
Jews, of which we also know from secular history, and had
sought refuge in Corinth. The Roman administration made no
distinction between Jews and Christian Jews. Paul and Silas too
had been brought before the magistrates at Philippi as Jews
(16: 20).

The history of the Christian Church owes much to this married couple. Paul writes of them in his letter to the Romans
(16: 3): " Greet Prisca and Aquila, my fellow workers in Christ
Jesus, who risked their necks for my life, to whom not only I
but also all the churches of the Gentiles give thanks." When
Paul puts the name of Prisca before that of her husband Aquila,

this is more than mere courtesy. This woman seems to have been a natural leader, in her personal activities, her determination and her theological aptitude. We shall hear of her in this chapter more than once.

To begin with, Paul and the married couple were brought together by their joint need of earning a living. He lives and works with them. They were " tentmakers " by trade. That is the meaning of the Greek. But whether it means that they actually made the material for tents or, as is more probable, prepared this material or leather for use, is not important. What we note with admiration here and elsewhere is that Paul is a worker in a workshop. Why does he do this? He himself tells us in his first letter to the Thessalonians which he wrote at Corinth: " Our appeal does not spring from terror or uncleanness, nor is it made with guile . . . We never used either words of flattery, as you know, or a cloak for greed, as God is witness . . . For you remember our labor and toil, brethren; we worked night and day, that we might not burden any of you, while we preached to you the gospel of God. You are witnesses, and God also, how holy and righteous and blameless was our behavior to you believers " (1 Thess. 2 : 3ff.).

Paul certainly let himself be supported by the churches in Macedonia (2 Cor. 11 : 9), and most of all by his favorite church at Philippi (Phil. 4 : 10ff.), but for the rest refused, in strict adherence to his basic principles, to accept any recompense for his service to the gospel. He is aware of the right of ministers of religion to be supported by the community (1 Cor. 9 : 4–14). But by refusing to avail himself of this right he wanted to show that his sole concern was for the gospel and not for any kind of human recompense or reward. Such an attitude was unusual, even in those early days of the Church's existence. But is it not true that the personal selflessness of the teachers and servants of the gospel has a more powerful effect than anything else on men who are searching for the truth? The Jewish rabbis who urged their pupils to learn a trade as well as study theology showed great wisdom.

Unsuccessful Attempts to Convert the Jews (18:4–6)

⁴And he argued in the synagogue every sabbath, and persuaded Jews and Greeks.

⁵When Silas and Timothy arrived from Macedonia, Paul was occupied with preaching, testifying to the Jews that the Christ was Jesus. ⁶And when they opposed and reviled him, he shook out his garments and said to them, " Your blood be upon your heads! I am innocent. From now on I will go to the Gentiles."

Paul everywhere remains faithful to his concern for the Jewish people. He means it quite seriously when he says, " I have great sorrow and unceasing anguish in my heart " (Rom. 9:1ff.). He cannot shake himself free of the wish to be himself " accursed and cut off from Christ for the sake of my brethren, my kinsmen by race." He is aware of the special calling of these people and the promises given to them from the time of Abraham. He refuses to be separated from them. He does not break under the many disappointments that his missionary efforts among the Jews have brought him. Despite persecution and ill treatment in the cities of Asia Minor and Macedonia, he makes his way in Corinth too to the synagogue on the sabbath and speaks to the Jews about Jesus. We assume that what he said to them resembled his speech to the Jews at Antioch of Pisidia (13:17–41).

And again he meets with incomprehension and opposition. Hard, hurtful words are hurled at him. " I will show him how much he must suffer for the sake of my name," the Lord had said in Damascus to Ananias (9:16). Paul is bitterly disappointed.

As at Antioch (13:51) he had shaken off the dust from his feet, so now at Corinth he shook out his garments and left the synagogue to its chosen destiny with words reminiscent of Pilate (Mt. 27:24): "Your blood be upon your head." Even though this painful anxiety for his own people will not leave him for the rest of his life, nevertheless in Corinth he feels freed from his responsibility for them and concentrates with his whole energy on his work with the Gentiles. The theological problem of the attitude of the Jews never ceases to concern him, and he is now beginning to formulate the ideas with which he sought to understand and explain the very different paths of Jews and Gentiles in the history of salvation. In the letter to the Romans (chapters 9–11) he will give profound theological expression to his ideas.

SUCCESS AMONG THE GENTILES (18:7–11)

⁷And he left there and went to the house of a man named Titius Justus, a worshiper of God; his house was next door to the synagogue. ⁸Crispus, the ruler of the synagogue, believed in the Lord, together with all his household; and many of the Corinthians hearing Paul believed and were baptized. ⁹And the Lord said to Paul one night in a vision, "Do not be afraid, but speak and do not be silent; ¹⁰for I am with you, and no man shall attack you to harm you; for I have many people in this city." ¹¹And he stayed a year and six months, teaching the word of God among them.

Externally too Paul shows that there has been a change in his activity. Next door to the synagogue is the house which becomes the center of his mission to the Gentiles. Titius Justus, its owner, was one of those who "feared God" and, though pagan, sought spiritual fulfillment in the Jewish religion. Now he and his companions hear the real message of salvation preached by Paul. Even the ruler of the synagogue was converted and became a Christian. His example must have influenced many. The conversion of men of importance has always drawn attention to the Church and brought further converts. The reverse is also true. The lapsing from the Church of such people causes dismay and spiritual unrest among the body of believers.

How difficult and discouraging the Apostle's work in Corinth must have been is shown most tellingly in the short sentence which describes the Lord's appearance in a vision at night. Again and again—in 22:18; 23:11 and elsewhere—the Apostle experiences these mysterious encounters with the risen Lord. Paul lived in a close personal relationship and union with the Lord who had called him. His letters witness to this also. In 2 Cor. 4:10 we read " Always carrying in the body the death of Jesus, so that the life of Jesus may also be manifested in our bodies." And in the same letter (12:8) he writes about his tormented body: " Three times I besought the Lord about this, that it should leave me; but he said to me, ' My grace is sufficient for you, for my power is made perfect in weakness.' "

We have to read the two letters to the Corinthians very carefully in order to understand Paul's situation at Corinth. In 1 Cor. 1:26ff. he writes: " Consider your call, brethren; not many of you were wise according to worldly standards, not many were powerful, not many were of noble birth; but God chose what is foolish in the world to shame the wise, God chose what is weak in the world to shame the strong, God chose what is low and despised in the world, even things that are not, to bring to nothing things that are." And in 1 Cor. 2:3ff. he confesses: " And I was with you in weakness and in much fear and trembling; and my speech and my message were not in plausible words of wisdom, but in demonstration of the Spirit and power, that your faith might not rest in the wisdom of men but in the power of God."

The Church at Corinth was, when all is said and done, a people easy to win over but not at all easy to keep together. This is clear to anyone who reads these letters carefully. The letters that have not come down to us, the " sorrowful " letters, for example (see 2 Cor. 2:3f.; 7:8), may contain things even more painful to read. Thus we can understand how the Lord wanted to encourage the Apostle, in Corinth especially, and assures Paul that he is with him and will protect him from all harm. In our admiration of the missionary work of the Apostle even as regards his physical achievements, we must not forget that this man who knew himself driven by a unique personal energy and zeal, was nevertheless only able to continue his work because a higher power helped and inspired him—the power of him who said: "Do not be afraid, but speak and do not be silent; for I am with you." These words remind us of the saying of the Old Testament prophets (Is. 41:10ff.; 45:5ff.), and of Jesus' words before and after his resurrection (Mt. 14:27; 17:7; 28:16ff.). Do we truly understand that all our efforts to preach Christ's message and bring his kingdom to realization derive their sense and meaning only from the presence of him who linked the promise of salvation to the commission he gave to his apostles when he said (Mt. 28:20): "Lo, I am with you always, to the close of the age."

BEFORE THE PROCONSUL GALLIO (18:12–17)

[12]*But when Gallio was proconsul of Achaia, the Jews made a united attack upon Paul and brought him before the tribunal.* [13]*saying, " This man is persuading men to worship God contrary to the law." * [14]*But when Paul was about to open his mouth,*

*Gallio said to the Jews, " If it were a matter of wrongdoing or
vicious crime, I should have reason to bear with you, O Jews;
¹⁵but since it is a matter of questions about words and names and
your own law, see to it yourselves; I refuse to be a judge of these
things." ¹⁶And he drove them from the tribunal. ¹⁷And they all
seized Sosthenes, the ruler of the synagogue, and beat him in
front of the tribunal. But Gallio paid no attention to this.*

Acts tells us very little of what Paul did in the " year and six
months " (18 : 11) of his first stay at Corinth. But the description
we are given here clearly sheds light on the situation for us.
Again the Jews appear as his real foes. We must distinguish
between two groups of Jews. 2 Cor. 11 : 22 tells us of a group
of Judaizers in the Church, who made difficulties for Paul, and
with whom he argues vehemently. But the Jews in Corinth
bitterly reject and oppose the Christian message as such and
joined battle there, as elsewhere, especially with Paul. These
Jews clearly realized that he was the most powerful and successful preacher and leader in the Church which was establishing
itself among the Gentiles.

Paul is brought before the Roman proconsul Gallio, who was
in charge of the province of Achaia. It was the first official confrontation between the Apostle and a leading representative of
the Roman authorities. There will be similar confrontations
later. Luke has a particular interest in depicting them. Gallio,
a noble, honorable and intellectual Roman, is brought face to
face with the preacher of the gospel. An inscription found at
Delphi tells us that the proconsul was in office in the year 50/51
or 51/52. This evidence gives powerful support to our chrono-
logy of Paul's activities. If we remember that Gallio was a
brother of the distinguished Roman philosopher Seneca, who
was the teacher of the Emperor Nero, it is especially easy to
believe in the rectitude of his attitude towards Paul when the

latter was brought before the tribunal. Paul and Gallio! In the year 65 Gallio together with his brother Seneca and another brother was to die, a victim of Nero's cruel capriciousness. Peter and Paul were to be the victims of the same Nero.

The accusation of the Jews seems to be deliberately two-sided. They accuse Paul of " persuading men to worship God contrary to the law." It is clear that they are thinking of the Jewish law and of the message of the Apostle as directed against their own teaching about salvation. But in the way they formulate the charge to the Romans they seem to be trying to turn it into a political one. The Romans gave legal recognition to certain cults, and forbade others. The Jewish religion is known to have been a " *religio licita* " in the Roman empire—a religion permitted by law. Since the early Christian churches consisted primarily of Jews, Christians could assume this privilege for themselves. But it is clear that the Jews of the continuously growing Church sought to oppose the Christians' right in this matter, and thus in Corinth they try to tell the tribunal that Paul's preaching was " contrary to the law." Again, as in the trial of Jesus, a religious circumstance is turned into a political one.

Gallio sees through their attempt. He knows that Paul's accusers are referring to purely internal Jewish matters, and refuses to be drawn in. Since he speaks of " words " and " names " which as judge do not concern him, we must assume that the accusation centered around the basic principles of Paul's teaching which was at the same time the main point of conflict between himself and the Jews—the question whether Jesus was the Messiah whom the Jews were expecting. Establishing this was an essential part of Paul's preaching to the Jews. But for the Jews it was the chief reason for their hostility.

Did Gallio reject their accusation more determinedly than Pilate had done in the case of Jesus? We know that Pilate was aware of the hidden motives of the Jews and that he wanted at first to have no part in their accusations against Jesus. But in the end he succumbed to their enormous pressure. It is true, of course, that a Roman judge would have been in a far more difficult position vis-à-vis the Jews in Jerusalem than a proconsul in Corinth.

The ruler of the synagogue was beaten before the eyes of Gallio. It is not clear whether it was the " Greeks " who were the attackers, perhaps out of anti-Jewish feelings, or whether " Greek " Jews wanted to give expression to their disappointment at the unsuccessful outcome of the case. Nor do we know whether this Sosthenes was identical with the one named in 1 Cor. 1 : 1. If he was, then we must assume that soon after this he joined the Church.

Another minor point arises here, and elsewhere too. It is concerned with the dating of Acts. Does it make much sense to place this encounter with Gallio as late as the year 80? Do we not have much more reason to assume—as used to be the case among exegetes—that Acts was written during Paul's trial, and that the story of Gallio and other similar occurrences were mentioned to show that Paul was the victim purely and simply of Jewish hostility, and was personally innocent as regards Roman law? Around the year 63, which would in that case be a possible date for Acts, Gallio was still in good standing with Nero, and his brother Seneca also.

RETURN TO ANTIOCH VIA EPHESUS (18:18–22)

[18]*After this Paul stayed away many days longer, and then took leave of the brethren and sailed for Syria, and with him Priscilla and Aquila. At Cenchreae he cut his hair, for he had a vow.* [19]*And they came to Ephesus, and he left them there; but he himself went into the synagogue and argued with the Jews.*

20When they asked him to stay for a longer period, he declined; 21but on taking leave of them he said, " I will return to you if God wills," and he set sail from Ephesus.

22When he had landed at Caesarea, he went up and greeted the church, and then went down to Antioch.

We are once more aware of the careful way in which Luke is writing his account. He lists the places on their return journey and thus brings back to its starting point an undertaking of the highest importance to the development of the Church. He sets sail from Cenchreae, the eastern harbour of Corinth. An important community seems to have arisen there. In Rom. 16.1 Paul names " our sister Phoebe, a deaconess of the church at Cenchreae."

The reader will find it strange to be told that Paul cut his hair at Cenchreae. It was a Jewish custom and concerned a religious vow. In the Mosaic law (Num. 6:2ff.) we read the following instructions: " When either a man or a woman makes a special vow, the vow of a Nazirite, to separate himself to the Lord, he shall separate himself from wine and strong drink . . . All the days of his separation he shall eat nothing that is produced by the grapevine . . . All the days of his vow of separation no razor shall come upon his head; until the time is completed for which he separates himself to the Lord, he shall be holy; he shall let the locks of hair of his head grow long." For the end of the period of the vow were also instructions (see Num. 6:13–21) about special offerings to be made in the temple at Jerusalem.

Thus Paul completes the period of his vow at Cenchreae. If we consider how urgently he explains in his letters to the Galatians and the Romans that they were no longer under the law, it is surprising that as a Christian he still follows what is only a religious custom. It is true that after his return from his third missionary journey he will once again take part in the closing rituals of such a vow (21 : 3), but the reasons there lie more in external consideration for the Jews at Jerusalem. Here however one has the impression that he is acting out of personal piety. Is this in contradiction to the teaching on the freedom from the law? Hardly. Even as a Christian he continued to regard as holy the Jewish prayers and religious customs so long as these were not considered necessary and effective—in an absolute sense—for man's salvation. In this behavior of Paul's we can see that any act performed in the right spirit is not contradictory to his basic thesis that it is not works that justify a man in the eyes of God but faith in Christ Jesus " apart from the law " (Rom. 3 : 21ff.).

We read with interest that he is accompanied as far as Ephesus by Priscilla and Aquila. It is a preparation for what we shall hear in the account that follows. Paul refuses to stay on in Ephesus at this time. But he will surely have found a great readiness for the gospel there and will make use of it on this third missionary journey, when he makes this town the center of his missionary activity for three years or so. He now lands at Caesarea and then we are told he " went up and greeted the church." This no doubt referred to Jerusalem—it was the usual expression for the journey to the holy city, and we are told that only after that did he go down to Antioch. What did he do in Jerusalem? We are tempted to think of the offering that was linked to the completion of his vow. Is it not somehow touching that this belligerent man who on his missionary travels was everywhere persecuted and ill-treated by the Jews in their attempt to safeguard Jewish orthodoxy, seeks out the holy city of the Jews in order to offer sacrifice out of an inner need? This surely moves us to remember how, with all inner loyalty to Church principle, we must nevertheless preserve an openness of mind and a love and respect for everything that seeks to worship God.

Paul's Third Missionary Journey (18:23—21:14)

The Teaching of Apollos (18:23-28)

²³After spending some time there he departed and went from place to place through the region of Galatia and Phrygia, strengthening all the disciples.

²⁴Now a Jew named Apollos, a native of Alexandria, came to Ephesus. He was an eloquent man, well versed in the scriptures. ²⁵He had been instructed in the way of the Lord; and being fervent in spirit, he spoke and taught accurately the things concerning Jesus, though he knew only the baptism of John. ²⁶He began to speak boldly in the synagogue; but when Priscilla and Aquila heard him, they took him and expounded to him the way of God more accurately. ²⁷And when he wished to cross to Achaia, the brethren encouraged him, and wrote to the disciples to receive him. When he arrived, he greatly helped those who through grace had believed, ²⁸for he powerfully confuted the Jews in public, showing by the scriptures that the Christ was Jesus.

We have here a small interruption in an account which otherwise concentrates exclusively on Paul. It concerns a very unusual figure. Acts speaks of him only once but for Paul, Apollos is no stranger. There may be good reason why Luke mentions him here and gives an account of him between the second and third missionary journeys. In the first letter to the Corinthians, which was written in Ephesus around 55 or 56 A.D. during Paul's third missionary journey, and thus after Apollos' work at Corinth, Paul says this of him—Apollos is in Ephesus at the time: " As for our brother Apollos, I strongly urged him to visit you with the other brethren, but it was not at all his will to come now. He will come when he has opportunity " (1 Cor. 16: 12).

Did Apollos ever again come to Corinth? Did Paul himself want him especially to do so? If one compares this text with what was said immediately before about Timothy, one becomes aware, despite the friendly words, of a certain reserve. Paul is personally well disposed towards Apollos. But he also knows that the latter's appearance at Corinth would not in every respect be to the benefit of the community. Paul will surely have agreed with the description given in Acts of Apollos, educated in the school of Alexandria, perhaps by the famous Jewish philosopher and theologian Philo, as " an eloquent man, well versed in the scriptures " who " greatly helped those who through grace had believed, for he powerfully confuted the Jews in public."

Nevertheless it was precisely this activity of Apollos that caused Paul real anxiety. We meet a human factor here that is inevitable in the situation—the reaction of certain groups within the church at Corinth. We read of it only indirectly in the early chapters of the first letter to the Corinthians. Paul speaks about " dissensions " in the community: " What I mean is that each one of you says, ' I belong to Paul,' or ' I belong to Apollos,' or ' I belong to Cephas,' or ' I belong to Christ ' " (1 Cor. 1:12). The Apostle names these four factions so as not to be referring too obviously to the division between his own party and that of Apollos. This is clear from later statements, for example in 1 Cor. 3:5: " What then is Apollos? What is Paul? Servants through whom you believed, as the Lord assigned to each. I planted, Apollos watered, but God gave the growth." And in 1 Cor. 4:6 we read: " I have applied all this to myself and Apollos for your benefit, brethren . . . that none of you may be puffed up in favor of one against another. For who sees anything different in you? What have you that you did not receive? If then you received it, why do you boast as if it were not a gift? "

It is very moving to read Paul's profound and compelling

explanations of the reasons why the Corinthians must not be influenced by purely material and superficial considerations regarding the work of Apollos but must come to an awareness of the essence of the gospel. He is surely thinking of Apollos when he writes in 1 Cor. 2:1ff.: "When I came to you, brethren, I did not come proclaiming to you the testimony of God in lofty words or wisdom. For I decided to know nothing among you except Jesus Christ and him crucified . . . And my speech and my message were not in plausible words of wisdom, but in demonstration of the Spirit and power, that your faith might not rest in the wisdom of men but in the power of God."

We have to keep the letter to the Corinthians in mind if we want to read the account in Acts with proper understanding. The two accounts do not contradict each other. According to Paul the work of Apollos was grace-aided and successful, like his own. But Paul's great concern for unity and accord within the Church forces him to point out to the Corinthians what were the really decisive elements in the work of this man who stood in the service of the gospel. We have no reason to assume the presence of personal disagreements or ordinary jealousy. It is true that Paul was not immune from human feelings—we see this here and there in his letters. But he makes honest attempts to let his work for Christ take precedence over every personal consideration.

We read with special interest that it was Priscilla and Aquila who, as loyal helpers in the missionary work of the primitive Church, concerned themselves with the instruction of Apollos in the fullness of the faith. Priscilla is mentioned first. Luke knows about the part of women in the saving work of the Church. In his gospel he is already most careful to list the names of women among the followers and helpers of Jesus.

We may be surprised to find Apollos who " knew only the baptism of John," preaching Christ's message. It is an example of the widespread religious movement started by the powerful preacher of repentance at the Jordan, of whom the gospels also tell us. Groups of the Baptist's adherents seem to have gathered in Alexandria, the birth place of Apollos, as well as in Ephesus. We read about the latter in 19:1ff. It will have taken time for the movement begun by the Baptist to be taken over completely by the growing Church of Christ. If we read the four gospels attentively, we see how careful they are to depict the person and significance of the Baptist in a relationship of proper subordination to the person and work of Jesus.

Paul in Ephesus (19:1–40)

ENCOUNTER WITH THE DISCIPLES OF JOHN (19:1–7)

¹*While Apollos was at Corinth, Paul passed through the upper country and came to Ephesus. There he found some disciples.* ²*And he said to them, " Did you receive the Holy Spirit when you believed? " And they said, " No, we have never even heard that there is a Holy Spirit." * ³*And he said, " Into what then were you baptized? " They said, " Into John's baptism." * ⁴*And Paul said, " John baptized with the baptism of repentance, telling the people to believe in the one who was to come after him, that is, Jesus." * ⁵*On hearing this, they were baptized in the name of the Lord Jesus.* ⁶*And when Paul had laid his hands upon them, the Holy Spirit came on them; and they spoke with tongues and prophesied.* ⁷*There were about twelve of them in all.*

On the second missionary journey, so we are told in 16:6, Paul was prevented from going to Asia and therefore to Ephesus. But now the way is clear. He will make Ephesus his missionary center for three years (19:8. 10; 20:31) and thus try to win over to the gospel the surrounding countryside. At this time churches were established at Colossae, Laodicea, Hierapolis (Col. 4:13) and surely also elsewhere. Paul also continued to keep in lively touch from Ephesus with the churches he had established earlier. The letter to the Galatians was probably written from Ephesus, and certainly the one we call the first letter to the Corinthians. We read in 1 Cor. 5:9 that this letter had been preceded by another that has not come down to us. In 2 Cor. 2:3f., and 7:8f., we find references to the so-called " sorrowful " letter. This too has not been preserved. From 2 Cor. 12:14 and 13:1 we must assume, even though nothing is said in Acts, that the Apostle briefly visited the Corinthian church during a crisis there, while staying at Ephesus. From all this we can see that the three years Paul spent at Ephesus were far more lively and troubled than the account in Acts allows us to suspect.

Ephesus, an intellectually and culturally important city, was inhabited by a mixed population of different races, countries and religions. To these belonged the " twelve " named in our text whom Paul met there. Like Apollos they were followers of the Baptist, yet they felt themselves to be Christian. We do not know how to explain this, since they had not received the Christian baptism. That they had never heard of the Holy Spirit is equally mysterious. As disciples of the Baptist, or even as believing Jews which they were, they must surely have had some knowledge, even if only in the Old Testament sense, of the Spirit of God. Thus their answer to Paul's question must be understood to mean that they knew nothing of the Holy Spirit as the one who belonged to the message of the gospel and was the special gift to men of the risen Lord. And because the mystery of the Spirit has a special relationship to baptism into Jesus Christ, Paul asks the question about their baptism and introduces them to the baptism of Christ.

The disciples of John at Ephesus were baptized " in the name of the Lord Jesus." We should like to know more about this. Who was the sponsor, what was the instruction given to those about to be baptized? Belief in the " Lord Jesus " was clearly the basis of their faith. In Peter's speech at Pentecost baptism is similarly referred to as being " in the name of Jesus Christ " (2 : 38). We cannot be sure whether this was the formula for valid baptism at the beginning of the Church's existence, or whether it was simply a phrase to distinguish Christian baptism from any other baptism. We leave open the possibility that the formula found in Matthew 28 : 19—" in the name of the Father and of the Son and of the Holy Spirit "—was already in use earlier than it might appear.

In baptizing, and especially in the laying on of hands by Paul, is revealed the mystery of the Holy Spirit. In texts like these we need not look for a logical arrangement of the Church's dogmatic teaching on sacraments. As we have already explained in our commentary on the baptism at Pentecost, the statements in Acts about the connection between baptism and the receiving of the Holy Spirit are not altogether clear. But in all important passages it is evident that baptism is the necessary basis for the coming of the Spirit. In our present text the laying on of hands by Paul is given special significance. It reminds us of Peter and John who, according to 8 : 14, laid hands in Samaria on those who had been baptized by Philip, so that they received the Holy Spirit. Luke is once again pointing to a deliberate parallel between Peter and Paul.

HE TURNS AWAY FROM THE JEWS AND PREACHES TO THE GENTILES (19 :8–10)

8And he entered the synagogue and for three months spoke boldly, arguing and pleading about the kingdom of God; 9but when some were stubborn and disbelieved, speaking evil of the Way before the congregation, he withdrew from them, taking the disciples with him, and argued daily in the hall of Tyrannus. [10]*This continued for two years, so that all the residents of Asia heard the word of the Lord, both Jews and Greeks.*

Paul's preaching to the Jews at Ephesus had as its theme the " kingdom of God." This was a concept familiar to them from the Old Testament. The history of Israel, as depicted in the sacred Scriptures, is the road to the kingdom of God. If we turn back in Acts to Paul's speech at Antioch of Pisidia (13 : 16ff.), we will get an idea of the way he must have presented the message of the kingdom of God to his Jewish listeners in the synagogue at Ephesus also. He begins his account of salvation history with the Jewish exodus from Egyptian slavery and goes on to David and finally to John the Baptist and the good news that, in the fullness of time, " what God promised to the fathers, this he has fulfilled." Jesus' death and resurrection will have been the central part of Paul's message in Ephesus also. He will have made his hearers aware of the tension between law and faith. If we assume that his letter to the Galatians was written in Ephesus, perhaps during the first days of his work there, then we may suppose that the theological arguments contained in this disputatious letter were largely developed during his confrontations with the local Jews.

Paul tried for " three months " to win their comprehension. But in Ephesus as elsewhere he continued to have the same experience. Again, as in Corinth (18 : 6f.) he departed from the synagogue and " argued daily in the hall of Tyrannus." We know nothing further of this Tyrannus but it is clear that Luke is continuing here too to give us basically reliable information. We can see from the farewell address which Paul delivers to the elders at Ephesus on his return journey that the Jews put the greatest obstacles in his way, even after this separation. He says in this address: " You yourselves know how I lived among you all the time from the first day that I set foot in Asia, serving the Lord with all humanity and with tears and with trials which befell me through the plots of the Jews " (20:18f.).

EXTRAORDINARY MIRACLES (19:11–22)

[11]And God did extraordinary miracles by the hands of Paul, [12]so that handkerchiefs or aprons were carried away from his body to the sick, and diseases left them and the evil spirits came out of them. [13]Then some of the itinerant Jewish exorcists undertook to pronounce the name of the Lord Jesus over those who had evil spirits, saying, " I adjure you by the Jesus whom Paul preaches." [14]Seven sons of a Jewish high priest named Sceva were doing this. [15]But the evil spirit answered them, " Jesus I know, and Paul I know; but who are you? " [16]And the man in whom the evil spirit was leaped on them, mastered all of them, and overpowered them, so that they fled out of that house naked and wounded.

The parallel between this passage and what we are told in 5:12ff. of Peter's powers of healing is obvious. We read there: " Many signs and wonders were done among the people by the hands of the apostles . . . they even carried out the sick into the streets, and laid them on beds and pallets, that as Peter came by at least his shadow might fall on some of them." Since Luke, the " physician " (Col. 4:14), reports these things, it is clear that he does not want to deny the beliefs current at that time about the mysterious healing powers of certain members of the Church.

We of course find it difficult to share views like these, though they were taken seriously at that time. But are we right? We may know a great deal about the primitive modes of thought of those days. But does this entitle us to reject out of hand the

mysterious powers that are said in our texts to witness to the
faith? Even if we cannot properly explain them, even if they
cannot be fitted into our rational everyday experience, have we
any right to doubt the existence of this combination of spiritual
and physical powers? Could it not be that we have lost the power
to sense the supernatural in the natural? In his gospel too, Luke
wrote about the mysterious powers of Jesus. We read there:
" All the crowd sought to touch him, for power came forth from
him and healed them all " (Lk. 6: 19). In Luke 8: 44 we are told
of the woman whose flow of blood ceased the moment she
touched the fringe of his garment. Must we classify all such
passages as creation myths? Would this be doing justice to the
message of the gospel?

We are moved by similar thoughts when we read the story of
the Jewish exorcists which, despite its serious theme, does not lack
a certain element of the comic. The story as it has been handed
down to us may go beyond the realm of the purely historical
by laying too great an emphasis on details instead of concen-
trating on the whole. But this does not justify our denying the
incident from beginning to end. We know from historical
sources that there were itinerant Jewish exorcists. We include
among them the figure of the Jewish magician Elymas Bar-Jesus,
of whom we are told in 13: 6f. What the encounter with the sons
of Sceva—a man otherwise not known to us—is intended to show
is the all-victorious power of Jesus which reveals itself as present
and effective precisely when there is an attempt to assume it
unjustly by external manipulation. Where there is no real belief
in Jesus' healing power but only external and egoistical motives,
there the powers hidden in the name of Jesus turn against the
man who tries to misuse them.

[17]*And this became known to all residents of Ephesus, both Jews
and Greeks; and fear fell upon them all; and the name of the*

Lord Jesus was extolled. [18]*Many also of those who were now believers came, confessing and divulging their practices.* [19]*And a number of those who practised magic arts brought their books together and burned them in the sight of all; and they counted the value of them and found it came to fifty thousand pieces of silver.* [20]*So the word of the Lord grew and prevailed mightily.*

We cannot help being reminded in this story about the man Simon Magus, of whom we are told in 8:9ff. With his " magic " he had for long " amazed the nation of Samaria " (8:11). But then he encounters another power, the power of the " good news about the kingdom of God and the name of Jesus Christ " and this power renders him powerless, though he had made himself out to be "great." The element of magic in antiquity is something altogether strange. Numerous magical texts and books with their curious formulae and invocations have come down to us. How should we think of them? They are evidence of primitive thought, of fraud and deception, of despair and longing, of lost and searching man. But is this the whole story? There is one thing we can clearly say about the text in question. Those who brought their magic books and burnt them understood, like Simon in Samaria, that he who opens himself to the saving power of Christ and the power of the Holy Spirit in faith and trust, need no longer depend on the dubious texts and invocations which men had used up to now in their groping awareness of the mysterious. Should such evidence of the power of the Spirit of Christ not give us pause for thought? Should it not bring to life and activity our faith which has been overlaid by rational thought?

Is it not significant that these extraordinary miracles of the Apostle, his cures, his exorcisms, prepare the way for Jesus' message and thus free men from the dark night and fantasies of their ignorance? " Fear fell upon them all; and the name of the

Lord Jesus was extolled . . . So the word of the Lord grew and prevailed mightily." We read these words with a troubled mind. Is our witness to this "word of the Lord" still sufficiently powerful to have something to say to those who listen to our theological and kerygmatic statements about Jesus? Can it bring them to repentance and wholesome fear? Where is the power of our words? Are our words really filled with the power of the Holy Spirit?

[21]*Now after these events Paul resolved in the Spirit to pass through Macedonia and Achaia and go to Jerusalem, saying, "After I have been there, I must also see Rome."* [22]*And having sent into Macedonia two of his helpers, Timothy and Erastus, he himself stayed in Asia for a while.*

This short passage, interrupting as it does the account of the Apostle's activity in Ephesus, seems rather curious. His task at Ephesus is still incomplete, yet he is already making new plans. He sees before him a mighty arc stretching from Ephesus across Macedonia, Greece and Jerusalem to Rome. He plans to revisit the churches he established during his second missionary journey. Among them is Philippi, his favorite church, but above all Corinth, the child of his sorrows. We can see from his letters to the Corinthians how urgently he wants to be with them once again. The two letters are at the same time evidence that over and above his pastoral anxiety he had a special reason for going to Macedonia and Greece, namely, the collection of contributions for the church at Jerusalem. 1 Cor. 16: 1–4 and especially 2 Cor. 8–9 discuss this urgently. For Paul too, Jerusalem is still the mother church.

Surprisingly, it is Rome that becomes his goal. In 23: 11 Paul is once more reminded of this. We read there that the "Lord" told him when in prison: "Take courage, for as you have testified about me at Jerusalem, so you must bear witness also at

Rome." The entire missionary account of Acts with its numerous stopping places and experiences seems ultimately to lead only to the one goal—Rome. In 28:14 we read: "And so we came to Rome," and it sounds like the fulfillment of a long cherished dream. In his letter to the Romans Paul shows a great longing for a meeting with the Roman church he praised so highly. The fact that the account in Acts makes such a point of moving in the direction of Rome, although Paul only arrived there as a prisoner, leads one to think that it was written with a Roman readership in mind and perhaps also with the idea of being helpful to the Apostle when a prisoner under Roman interrogation—assuming, of course, that Luke wrote his book while Paul was still alive. But exegetes are not greatly inclined to this view at the present time.

Uproar among the Silversmiths (19:23–41)

²³About that time there arose no little stir concerning the Way. ²⁴For a man named Demetrius, a silversmith, who made silver shrines of Artemis, brought no little business to the craftsmen. ²⁵These he gathered together, with the workmen of like occupation, and said, "Men, you know that from this business we have our wealth. ²⁶And you see and hear that not only at Ephesus but almost throughout all Asia this Paul has persuaded and turned away a considerable company of people, saying that gods made with hands are not gods. ²⁷And there is danger not only that this trade of ours may come into disrepute but also that the temple of the great goddess Artemis may count for nothing, and that she may even be deposed from her magnificence, she whom all Asia and the world worship."

²⁸When they heard this they were enraged, and cried out, "Great is Artemis of the Ephesians!" ²⁹So the city was filled with the confusion; and they rushed together into the theater, dragging with them Gaius and Aristarchus, Macedonians who were Paul's companions in travel. [30]*Paul wished to go in among the crowd, but the disciples would not let him;* [31]*some of the Asiarchs also, who were friends of his, went to him and begged him not to venture into the theater.* [32]*Now some cried one thing, and some another; for the assembly was in confusion, and most of them did not know why they had come together.* [33]*Some of the crowd prompted Alexander, whom the Jews had put forward. And Alexander motioned with his hand, wishing to make a defense to the people.* [34]*But when they recognized that he was a Jew, for about two hours they all with one voice cried out, "Great is Artemis of the Ephesians!"* [35]*And when the town clerk had quieted the crowd, he said, "Men of Ephesus, what man is there who does not know that the city of the Ephesians is temple keeper of the great Artemis, and the sacred stone that fell from the sky?* [36]*Seeing then that these things cannot be contradicted, you ought to be quiet and do nothing rash.* [37]*For you have brought these men here who are neither sacrilegious nor blasphemers of our goddess.* [38]*If therefore Demetrius and the craftsmen with him have a complaint against any one, the courts are open, and there are proconsuls; let them bring charges against one another.* [39]*But if you seek anything further, it shall be settled in the regular assembly.* [40]*For we are in danger of being charged with rioting today, there being no cause that we can give to justify this commotion."* [41]*And when he had said this, he dismissed the assembly.*

This passage is unusually detailed for Acts. We might ask why such detail? Looked at theologically, the text is not especially informative. Would the reader not have preferred to have been given a fuller account of the, for the most part very brief, discussions in the Jewish synagogues? And yet, we should not like to do without this colorful episode. Luke is a Hellenist, a personal friend of the Apostle. He is concerned with depicting the world encountered by Paul and the Church in the most pleasing way possible. Even though the passage bears every trace of Luke's literary style, and he was an author who knew how to bring such an account to life, it is nevertheless based, like so much else in the book, on accurate information. The Macedonians Gaius and Aristarchus seem to have been Luke's informants —they are cited as witnesses in 19:29. In 20:5 Aristarchus, a Macedonian from Thessalonia, is named as one of the companions of Paul, among whom Luke must also have been, since the account is in the first person plural. And according to 27:2 Aristarchus was also present when the prisoner Paul was taken to Rome. With him, as we see from the use of the first person plural and the account in Col. 4:10. 14, was Luke. Thus the latter had access to reliable information about the stormy meeting of the silversmiths at Ephesus.

Two things especially strike us here. From the point of view of the history of religion, what we note above all is the careful description of the Greeks' belief in idols and of associated cults. And from the point of view of psychology, we note how convincingly the behavior of Demetrius and his fellow craftsmen is shown to represent a universal human reaction.

Literature and archeology confirm for us the existence of a widespread Ephesian cult of the goddess Artemis. Her great temple was accounted one of the seven wonders of the world. We know of her shrine and her famous image in which were blended the features of the Phyrgian mother goddess Cybele and the Greek virgin goddess of hunting. In the cult of the Ephesian goddess Artemis we have a very fine example of the combination of eastern and western ideas and piety. Ephesus possessed other shrines too, but the temple of Artemis outshone them all, and thousands of pilgrims flocked to it yearly. The belief of these people, harking back to times immemorial, fed from a variety of sources, borne up by their longing and striving after the unattainable, quite naturally sought refuge and support in the eye-catching splendor of this temple and its legendary fame. They came to Ephesus and to other famous places of pilgrimage in the Hellenistic world out of genuine religious need and trust.

This was the world encountered by Paul. It was not a world of primitive paganism, as we like to think, but of religious feeling rooted in daily life. It was a world bound up, it is true, with a suspect polytheism, but this gives us no right to doubt the genuineness and seriousness of those who brought their troubles and hopes to the goddess. We can see how difficult it must have been for the Apostle to preach Jesus' message of salvation, his cross and resurrection, to this tightly knit religious world. It must have seemed hopeless. Yet Paul had great success there, and the reason lay in what we have just been told about the power of the Holy Spirit made manifest in the Apostle's extraordinary miracles—his victories over sickness and evil spirits—which went far beyond anything the devotees of the Ephesian Artemis were able to relate about their own goddess.

The other element we find so convincing in this account is the existence of the profit motive which drove Demetrius and his companions so cleverly and perhaps only half-convincingly to make use of the religious feelings of the time for their own business purposes. The buying and selling of devotional articles is universal in every age and every cult. Such articles were manufactured in Ephesus on a large scale in order to provide pilgrims with an opportunity of acquiring inexpensive mementoes of their pilgrimage in the form of small replicas of the shrine of Artemis and of the image of the goddess. None of this is difficult to understand. But as the sale of these objects decreased, so it became obvious that the craftsmen felt themselves endangered, and gathered together to protest. Demetrius cunningly disguised his motives by pretending concern for the cult of the goddess, when in reality it was concern for his business that lay at the back of his mind. Such behavior is not unusual in the world today.

There must have been many other occasions of wild uproar in the theater at Ephesus. It lay in the middle of the city and held 25,000 people. The foundations are still standing. Against whom were these excited men protesting? They had dragged with them two of Paul's companions. A Jew wishes to speak. Did he intend by his defense to separate himself from Paul? It appears so. But all he succeeds in doing is release noisy shouts on behalf of the goddess Artemis. For two hours the shouts continue—a scene which in its changeable nature holds a memorable place in the history of the Church.

The unnamed " town clerk," clearly a leading official of the city, quietens the crowd in an intelligent and forceful way. He plays effectively upon the pride of the Ephesians in their city, pays due attention to their concern for the temple of Artemis, and with a carefully considered warning of the strictness of the Roman administration, he leads them back to the proper path for dealing with these and similar questions. What was his attitude towards Paul personally? Was he a friend of his, like the " Asiarchs " referred to in 19:31 who, as officials of the province, had been appointed by Rome to watch over its peace and order? Did Luke make a point of stressing the reasonableness of these Ephesian officials because he wanted to make it clear, here as elsewhere, how favorable was the attitude towards Paul of those who were in the service of Rome?

Macedonia and Greece; Return to Jerusalem (20:1—21:14)

THROUGH MACEDONIA TO GREECE (20:1-3a)

[1]*After the uproar ceased, Paul sent for the disciples and having exhorted them took leave of them and departed for Macedonia.*

²*When he had gone through these parts and had given them much encouragement, he came to Greece.* ³ᵃ*There he spent three months . . .*

If we glance at the second letter to the Corinthians, we shall have a more realistic understanding of the passage we have just been reading. 2 Corinthians shows us that it was his anxiety for the turbulent church at Corinth, quite apart from other considerations, which impelled Paul to make his way to Greece. We have already seen that he must have paid a brief visit to Corinth on an earlier occasion during his stay at Ephesus, for 2 Cor. 13:1 speaks of his going there for the "third time." The same letter also tells us that Paul had in the meantime sent Titus to Corinth with a special commission—presumably the sorrowful letter (2 Cor. 2:4)—and was awaiting his return with great impatience. We read in 2 Cor. 2:12f.: "When I came to Troas to preach the gospel of Christ, a door was opened for me in the Lord; but my mind could not rest because I did not find my brother Titus there. So I took leave of them and went to Macedonia." And in 2 Cor. 7:5 we read: "For even when we came into Macedonia, our bodies had no rest but we were afflicted at every turn—fighting without and fear within. But God, who comforts the downcast, comforted us by the coming of Titus."

In the same letter (2 Cor. 1:8f.) he refers to his earlier experiences at Ephesus: "We do not want you to be ignorant, brethren, of the affliction we experienced in Asia; for we were so utterly, unbearably crushed that we despaired of life itself. Why, we felt that we had received the sentence of death; but that was to make us rely not on ourselves but on God who raises the dead."

Thus we can see that the uproar among the silversmiths, which Acts describes, was not the only experience of hostility and persecution he had to undergo at Ephesus. The following sentence from the first letter to the Corinthians (15:32), which he wrote from Ephesus, is very revealing: " What do I gain if, humanly speaking, I fought with beasts at Ephesus? "

After receiving the good news about Titus (2 Cor. 7:7), Paul left Macedonia for Greece, where he remained " three months " —presumably during the winter of 57/58, though some say 55/56 (1 Cor. 16:6). We have to remember that at the end of that time he wrote his unique letter to the Romans where he summarized and brought together in all their profundity the principal ideas contained in his teaching on salvation.

RETURN THROUGH MACEDONIA TO TROAS AND MILETUS (20:3b–16)

³ᵇ*And when a plot was made against him by the Jews as he was about to set sail for Syria, he determined to return through Macedonia. ⁴Sopater of Beroea, the son of Pyrrhus, accompanied him; and of Thessalonians, Aristarchus and Secundus; and Gaius of Derbe, and Timothy; and the Asians, Tychicus and Trophimus. ⁵These went on and were waiting for us at Troas, ⁶but we sailed away from Philippi after the days of Unleavened Bread, and in five days we came to them at Troas, where we stayed for seven days.*

⁷*On the first day of the week, when we were gathered together to break bread, Paul talked with them, intending to depart on the morrow; and he prolonged his speech until midnight. ⁸There were many lights in the upper chamber where we were gathered. ⁹And a young man named Eutychus was sitting in the window. He sank into a deep sleep as Paul talked still longer; and being overcome by sleep, he fell down from the third story and was taken up dead. ¹⁰But Paul went down and bent over him, and*

embracing him said, " Do not be alarmed, for his life is in him."
[11]And when Paul had gone up and had broken bread and eaten,
he conversed with them a long while, until daybreak, and so
departed. [12]And they took the lad away alive, and were not a
little comforted.

Again the Jews try to disrupt the work of the Apostle. Presumably they planned to overpower him at sea. For we know from
the accounts that follow how they repeatedly tried to ambush
him while a prisoner (23:12ff.; 25:3). The Apostle learns about
the intention of the Jews and takes the safer though longer cross-
country route through Macedonia.

The list of his seven companions is surprising in its detail. Had
he memorized all the names? Or did he keep a journal of their
travels? The records that follow seem to have been taken from
such a journal. And in 20:5 the account is once again recognis-
ably in the first person plural. Why are we told about these
people here? The majority of them are also mentioned elsewhere
in Acts and in Paul's letters. The reason is the collections made
by Paul in Macedonia and Greece for the support of the mother
church at Jerusalem.

In 2 Corinthians 8–9 we have grateful references to the
generosity of the Macedonians. There too the Corinthians are
encouraged to emulate them. We also see the Apostle's concern
about this in the letter to the Romans which he wrote immediately before his departure from Corinth. There he said: " At
present, however, I am going to Jerusalem with aid for the
saints. For Macedonia and Achaia have been pleased to make
some contribution for the poor among the saints at Jerusalem ...
When therefore I have completed this, and have delivered to
them what has been raised, I shall go on by way of you to
Spain . . . I appeal to you, Brethren . . . to strive together
with me in your prayers to God on my behalf, that I may be

delivered from the unbelievers in Judea, and that my service for Jerusalem may be acceptable to the saints " (Rom. 15:25ff.).

A curious fear emerges from these words. We know that the eagerness shown by the Apostle for organizing these collections was looked on with dislike and even mistrust by certain members of the early Church, especially in Jerusalem. Thus we can understand it when he says in 1 Cor. 16:3f.: "When I arrive, I will send those whom you accredit by letter to carry your gift to Jerusalem. If it seems advisable that I should go also, they will accompany me." Still clearer are the statements in 2 Cor. 8:18ff., where Paul refers to an unnamed " brother " and says, with an eye to the proposed collection, that he is sending this man " who is famous among all the churches for his preaching of the gospel; and not only that, but he has been appointed by the churches to travel with us in this gracious work which we are carrying, for the glory of the Lord and to show our good will. We intend that no one should blame us about this liberal gift which we are administering, for we aim at what is honorable not only in the Lord's sight but also in the sight of men."

If we weigh these words carefully and put them into their proper context, it is not difficult to understand that Paul was taking proper precautions on his return journey to Jerusalem, when he was carrying with him the proceeds of the collections, and was taking with him as his companions the men named in this passage who were also representatives of the churches. We must count Luke among these. Although he is not listed by name, we know that he is there from the use of the first person plural, which begins in 20:5 and continues, sometimes more clearly, sometimes less, to the end of the book. The account in the first person plural begins at Philippi, and this was also the town where previously the first person plural account came to an end (16:17). We can deduce from this that Luke was closely connected with the church there and was perhaps even its repre-

sentative in the matter of the collections, and accompanied Paul
as such.

We cannot tell from the text whether Paul celebrated the
Jewish Pasch as a Christian Easter or not, when he was with the
church at Philippi with whom, according to his letter to them,
he had a close relationship. We know nothing about the beginnings of the Christian Easter. It is possible that the intention here
is only to fix the date. This is done several times in Acts by
means of the Jewish calendar (2:1; 12:3; 27:9).

The stop at Troas, which lasted seven days, gives us much
food for thought. Troas has a special place in Paul's work. In
16:8f. we are told that it was there that Paul, in a vision at
night, was called to preach the gospel in Macedonia. In 2 Cor.
2:12 Paul writes that "door was opened" for him "in the
Lord" at Troas, but that he could not find the time to stay there
because of his anxiety about Corinth and about Titus whom he
had sent there. Now he seizes the opportunity to pay special
regard to the church at Troas.

"On the first day of the week" he met together with the
community "to break bread." The "first day of the week" is
closely linked in the New Testament with the witness to the
mystery of Jesus' resurrection. The resurrection made the first
day of the week, our Sunday, holy to believers. It replaced the
Jewish Sabbath. We can see how this day was celebrated as the
"day of the Lord" on which the Church assembled together to
worship him. Apart from this passage, the special character of the
day is also shown in 1 Cor. 16:2 and in Revelation 1:10. But we
know little about the liturgical aspect of the celebration. The
"ministry of the word" (6:4), the preaching of salvation and
the eucharistic meal were part of the weekly celebration from the
beginning. "Breaking bread together" can refer to the communal love feast of believers, but in our account it refers
specifically to the eucharistic meal. Though the boundaries be-

tween the love meal and the " eucharistic meal " may still have been fluid, the warning given by the Apostle in 1 Cor. 11 : 17ff. shows us how solemnly the early Church regarded the special character of the eucharistic meal.

Luke's particular reason for mentioning the breaking of bread at Troas was to tell the story of the young man through whom the Apostle was able to show his kerygmatic power. The passage reads like the clearly recollected account of an eye-witness. Luke knows the name of the young man, Eutychus; he remembers the " many lights in the upper chamber." And he may also be remembering the length of the Apostle's speech since he writes that " he prolonged his speech until midnight " and talked " still longer." We cannot of course be completely certain that the young man who was " overcome by sleep " and " fell down from the third story " was really dead, but the account does seem to be referring to a real raising from the dead. The Apostle's attitude seems to intend this. We are inclined to see in the miracle another parallelism with the raising that is attributed to Peter in 9 : 36ff. Both episodes have certain details in common. The words spoken by Paul remind us of Jesus' words at the raising of Jairus' daughter (Mark 5 : 39). If we see the story of Troas as an eye witness account, then all attempts at demythologizing, at explaining the episode in theological or symbolic terms, become irrelevant, and we take the event to be a confirmation of what we read in Mark 16 : 20 : " And they went forth and preached everywhere, while the Lord worked with them and confirmed the message by signs that attended it."

¹³But going ahead to the ship, we set sail for Assos, intending to take Paul aboard there; for so he had arranged, intending himself to go by land. ¹⁴And when he met us at Assos, we took him on board and came to Mitylene. ¹⁵And sailing from there we came the following day opposite Chios; the next day we touched

at Samos; and the day after that we came to Miletus. [16]*For Paul*
had decided to sail past Ephesus, so that he might not have to
spend time in Asia; for he was hastening to be at Jerusalem, if
possible, on the day of Pentecost.

Only a traveler's diary could provide such exact information
about dates and stopping places. We are not told why Paul, who
was clearly the leader of the expedition, sent his companions on
ahead by ship but himself went by the shorter route to Assos on
foot. The map shows it to have been a distance of about 25 miles.
It is astonishing how the frequently sick Apostle was able to
take the long and presumably arduous route across the peninsula
after the exhausting time he had spent at Troas and the final all-
night session there. Did he want to be on his own? We can only
be amazed in face of so much energy, such iron will and solid
achievements.

Why was he in such a hurry to be at Jerusalem for Pentecost?
Was it because of the Jewish festival that brought innumerable
pilgrims there from every country? It would hardly have been a
question of a Christian celebration of Pentecost. The word
" Pentecost " is perhaps used here, as in 1 Cor. 16:8, only to put
a date on his arrival. The reference to Pentecost is first and foremost an indication of the haste, which did not allow him
sufficient time during his return journey to re-visit his missionary
center at Ephesus, but forced him to " sail past." Was it really
only pressure of time that prevented him from visiting Ephesus?
If we read the relevant texts in the second letter to the
Corinthians, we can understand how Paul did not want to feel
himself once again under " the sentence of death " from which
" God who raises the dead " had delivered him (2 Cor. 1:9f.).
But the following passage vividly describes his great anxiety
about Ephesus.

FAREWELL ADDRESS IN MILETUS TO THE ELDERS OF THE CHURCH OF EPHESUS (20:17–38)

¹⁷*And from Miletus he sent to Ephesus and called to him the elders of the church.* ¹⁸*And when they came to him, he said to them :*

" *You yourselves know how I lived among you all the time from the first day that I set foot in Asia,* ¹⁹*serving the Lord with all humility and with tears and with trials which befell me through the plots of the Jews;* ²⁰*how I did not shrink from declaring to you anything that was profitable, and teaching you in public and from house to house,* ²¹*testifying both to Jews and to Greeks of repentance to God and of faith in our Lord Jesus Christ.* ²²*And now, behold, I am going to Jerusalem, bound in the Spirit, not knowing what shall befall me there;* ²³*except that the Holy Spirit testifies to me in every city that imprisonment and afflictions await me.* ²⁴*But I do not account my life of any value nor as precious to myself, if only I may accomplish my course and the ministry which I received from the Lord Jesus, to testify to the gospel of the grace of God.* ²⁵*And now, behold, I know that all you among whom I have gone about preaching the kingdom will see my face no more.* ²⁶*Therefore I testify to you this day that I am innocent of the blood of all of you,* ²⁷*for I did not shrink from declaring to you the whole counsel of God.* ²⁸*Take heed to yourselves and to all the flock, in which the Holy Spirit has made you guardians, to feed the church of the Lord which he obtained with his own blood.* ²⁹*I know that after my departure fierce wolves will come in among you, not sparing the flock;* ³⁰*and from among your own selves will arise men speaking perverse things, to draw away the disciples after them.* ³¹*Therefore be alert, remembering that for three years I did not cease night or day to admonish every one with tears.* ³²*And now, I commend you to God and to the word of his grace, which is able to build you up and to give you the inheritance among all those who are sanctified.* [33]*I coveted no one's silver or gold or apparel.* [34]*You yourselves know that these hands ministered to my necessities, and to those who were with me.* [35]*In all things I have shown you that by so toiling one must help the weak, remembering the words of the Lord Jesus, how he said, ' It is more blessed to give than to receive.' "*

[36]*And when he had spoken thus, he knelt down and prayed with them all.* [37]*And they all wept and embraced Paul and kissed him,* [38]*sorrowing most of all because of the word he had spoken, that they should see his face no more. And they brought him to the ship.*

We have deliberately quoted this passage in its entirety, without dividing it up into sections. For it must be read in the context of the whole, before one can single out individual statements for comment. We have here one of the most lively and informative speeches in Acts. Even though the author of Acts has given his own individual style to the shape and form of this and other speeches, we get the impression that he has convincingly recreated the actual situation and that it represents the true recollections of one whom we know, from the use of the first person plural, to have been an eye-witness. The attentive reader will also notice that this speech, which is the only speech made by Paul in front of leading members of the Church and reproduced in Acts in quite this length, contains many statements and themes that remind us of Paul's letters. This in itself is evidence that what we have before us here is in essence an utterance by Paul.

This farewell speech has its carefully chosen place in the structure of Acts as a whole. Even though it is addressed to a special audience, the men of Ephesus, it is a very moving summary not only of the Apostle's missionary work in Ephesus, but of the entire development of the Church up to that time. And as we are about to see, this speech also completes the account of the Apostle's work in Acts, which now goes on to discuss his long imprisonment. In the men of Ephesus Paul sees all those whom he has met as " servant of Jesus Christ, called to be an apostle, set apart for the gospel of God " (Rom. 1 : 1), in order to preach to them the gospel of salvation.

The fact that Paul summoned the elders of Ephesus and, according to 20 : 18. 25, of the neighboring churches also, to Miletus which was about 40 miles away, is not only proof of his ceaseless care for these earlier missionary places and a sign of the loyalty of his followers there, but also an act of his apostolic power which impels him, as " minister of Christ Jesus to the Gentiles " (Rom. 15 : 15f.), to feel himself responsible and competent to act for them all. He writes as follows to the church at Rome: " I am under obligation both to Greeks and to barbarians, both to the wise and to the foolish " (Rom. 1 : 14). And in 2 Cor. 11 : 28 he speaks about the " daily pressure upon me of my anxiety for all the churches." The speech itself, despite its over-riding theme of loving concern for his flock, is permeated with the consciousness of apostolic authority, and also with prophetic knowledge of what is to come. It contains statements of principle regarding the demands of pastoral and ecclesiastical office which remain valid and meaningful for us today.

If we consider the individual themes contained in the speech, we shall note the significance, both as regards the Apostle's work and the motivation of Acts as such, of the sentence where we are told of " trials " which befell Paul " through the plots of the Jews." It was the Jews who had become for him an " affliction " (2 Cor. 1 : 8) here in Asia, as elsewhere in his work. They turned his service to a service with " tears." When we read this, we are reminded of all the statements with which

Paul's letters describe his efforts on behalf of the gospel. He was a " servant " of the Lord Jesus Christ (Rom. 1:1; Gal. 1:10; Phil. 1:1; 2:22), " with all humility " (cf. 2 Cor. 10:12; 11:7; 12:9ff., etc.); in " toil and hardship," as he so movingly relates in 2 Cor. 11:23ff. (Cf. 2:4; Gal. 4:19f.).

Paul gave them the message of salvation unadorned and in its fullness, as he declares in the next verse. And in verse 26f. he asserts still more movingly, almost like an incantation : " Therefore I testify to you this day that I am innocent of the blood of all of you, for I did not shrink from declaring to you the whole counsel of God." Why does the Apostle put such a stress on this? It sounds like an answer to a criticism, like one justifying himself in face of an unjust attack. He speaks as a pastor of souls, as one who feels himself responsible for those in his charge. The departing Apostle, like all who are in a position of responsibility towards others, could not refrain from anxiously wondering whether he had done everything possible to lead those others to the goal to which they had been called. Again and again it becomes a question of whether the messenger of the gospel has preached the will of God—even when it seemed inopportune and unacceptable—clearly and unambiguously, without diminishment or distortion of the truth, without human consideration for himself or others.

" I do not shrink from . . . teaching you in public and from house to house, testifying both to Jews and Greeks of repentance to God and of faith in our Lord Jesus Christ." The methods and aims of the pastoral office are clearly seen in these words. Paul is called and he is sent. As an apostle he does not sit back and wait for men to come to him, he goes after them; he seeks them out and urges them to an external and internal confrontation with the gospel, the " power of God for salvation " (Rom. 1:16). The account in Acts has so far shown this clearly. In Athens Paul went to the market place and spoke to the Greeks; in the synagogue he spoke to the Jews. And his message was " testimony," not skilled theology or presumptuous knowledge, but testimony witnessing to what he himself, the preacher, was most deeply and movingly committed to, testimony to the experience of the Spirit and of grace. He wanted to convert men from their sin and error—Jews as well as Greeks. For they all " fall short of the glory of God " (Rom. 3:23), and are dependent on saving "faith in our Lord Jesus Christ." For Paul there is only one way to God, through Jesus Christ our Lord. If we have some small acquaintance with the Apostle's letters, above all the letter to the Romans, then we shall recognize the genuine Pauline voice speaking to us in this sentence of his farewell address.

The Apostle now turns from the past to the future. He thinks of the way he has to go. Jerusalem is his goal. He does not know what will befall him there but has a prophetic foreknowledge : " The Holy Spirit testifies to me in every city that imprisonment and afflictions await me." Even though we have not so far been told of private revelations like those mentioned in 21:4. 11ff., this does not exclude the reality of such events. " Imprisonment and afflictions " belong to the life of him about whom it was said: " I will show him how much he must suffer for the sake of my name " (9:16). Again we must read his letters, above all the second letter to the Corinthians, to understand the mystery of the suffering which has been part of his life since Damascus.

Paul fully understands the meaning of the path he has chosen. He does not account his earthly life " of any value." His one and only real desire is expressed in the following words: " If only I may accomplish my course [as though it were a running race] and the ministry which I received from the Lord Jesus, to testify to the gospel of the grace of God." These words reveal not only the principal theme of Paul's theology but also the passionate way in which he expresses himself. It is not necessary to discuss this in detail with the reader who has read his letters.

Men have rightly recognized the strong similarity between Paul's path as stated here and the way in which Jesus' own path to his passion in Jerusalem is described in the gospels. We think of the thrice repeated prophetic assertion of his suffering, and of the meaning given to this suffering by Jesus.

Paul goes on his way, " bound in the Spirit." He knows himself to be bound, he is not the master of his own destiny. He has given himself over to him who, since Damascus and since Antioch, has taken command of him, the Holy Spirit who is the " Spirit of God " and at the same time the " Spirit of Christ " (Rom. 8:9f.). In 13:2 we read that the Holy Spirit set him apart for the work to which he had called him. " Being sent out by the Holy Spirit " (13:4), he began his mission, and the Spirit remained with him. As a prisoner is bound to his guard, so Paul knows that in all the circumstances of his life he is bound to the Spirit. Knowing in advance what will befall him, he knows that his hearers, the elders of Ephesus and many others who are listening to his farewell speech, would see his face no more." And at these words, as we are told in 20:37f., " they all wept."

Verse 28 contains a sentence of great importance for the theology of the church. Paul speaks of the function and responsibility of those who have care of the " church of the Lord." The twofold being of the Church, human and divine, is strikingly expressed in an image often used in the Bible, that of " flock " and " shepherd." The elders of the Church are called " bishops." This word does not as yet refer to a strictly hierarchical office. Literally it means guardians, keepers, watchmen. The reason for their appointment does not lie in their own decision or in the will of the community, though both these play a part in it, but in the Holy Spirit who has made them " guardians." And this gives their office a special value.

The " church of God," too, was not established purely as a result of human decision and agreement. The Lord " obtained " it " with his own blood." We know whose blood it was, the blood of Jesus, " whom God put forward as an expiation by his blood, to be received by faith " (Rom. 3:25). We recognize here the principal elements of the Pauline doctrine of salvation. The " church of God " derives its dignity and indeed its existence from the acts of God's mercy towards men through his Son, and from the willingness of men to believe the promises of God. Do we really understand the true meaning of the Church? Are we aware of the real meaning of the task of guiding the flock of the Lord?

Paul sees " fierce wolves " breaking into the flock. This image is common in the New Testament. It comes from the experience of shepherds. The Sermon on the Mount (Mt. 7:15) warns of those who will come in "sheep's clothing but inwardly are ravenous wolves." In the parable of the " good shepherd " (Jn. 10:12) we are told of the " hireling " who looks after the sheep, and " sees the wolf coming and flees; and the wolf snatches them and scatters them." Paul points to the persecutors who will oppress the churches from without. He may be thinking of the Jews especially. But the danger which comes from within the Church and with false teaching brings quarrels and dissensions is far more serious. Church history has over the course of centuries been a sad commentary on this prophecy, which sprang from the already painful experience of the primitive Church.

" Therefore be alert," is the departing Apostle's warning to all into whose hands he places his work. This call to watchfulness appears in all the writings of the New Testament. It is the call to men living at the close of the age. " Watch therefore—for you do not know when the master of the house will come . . . And what I say to you I say to all: Watch "—thus Jesus warns them in his eschatological speech in Mark 13:25ff. And in the Apostle's letters this admonition recurs again and again. In the first letter to the Thessalonians (1 Thess. 5:6) he writes: " Let us keep awake and be sober." This warning is valid for all those who are called by the Lord, but most particularly for those to whom is entrusted not only their own salvation but that of others. In the letter to the Hebrews (13:17) there is reference to the " leaders . . . keeping watch over your souls, as men who will have to give account."

Paul reminds them of his own example. In the three years he spent working at Ephesus, he did not stop watching. " I do not cease night or day to admonish everyone with tears." In 2 Cor. 11:27 he speaks of " many a sleepless night " and in 1 Thess. 2:9 we read: " You remember our labor and toil, brethren: we worked night and day, that we might not burden any of you, while we preached to you the gospel of God." The Apostle earned his own and his companions' keep by his own work, and it must have been very moving when he showed them in Miletus his work-worn hands. These hands were witnesses to his selfless-ness and honesty, his renunciation of money and possessions and of all material advantages. He bases this renunciation on a say-ing of the Lord given only here, not in the gospels, and thus points to the guiding principle which, at any rate in spirit, ought to motivate all those appointed to ecclesiastical office.

One sentence has been omitted here, for the sake of a con-nected argument. But now we must consider it or we shall be overlooking an essential aspect of Paul's pastoral teaching. The sentence reads as follows: " And now I commend you to God and to the words of his grace, which is able to build you up and to give you the inheritance among all those who are sanctified." All admonitions and directions, all principles of action springing from human thought and experience, are useless and ineffective if the all-fulfilling power of God does not take hold of wavering, ignorant man and bring him into the mysterious realm of grace. Paul speaks of the " word of his grace." This expression conceals various layers of meaning but in the last analysis stands for the gospel of God, the gospel in the widest and fullest sense. This gospel is the " word " of his grace, for it reveals the saving grace of the merciful God. But it is also grace itself and gives grace to all who open themselves in trusting faith to the message of salvation which comes to us in Christ Jesus and in his life-giving words.

" The word of his grace . . . is able to build you up." What is meant is the " building up " of which Paul speaks in 2 Cor. 5:17: " If anyone is in Christ, he is a new creation; the old has passed away, behold, the new has come." In Christ we are living according to a new principle; we are taken up into the mysterious life of the triune God. We are numbered among the " saints," for " he has delivered us from the dominion of darkness and transferred us to the kingdom of his beloved Son " (Col. 1:13). And thus we have been given a glorious " inheritance." For according to Rom. 8:29 this Son is the " first-born among many brethren " and we are united with him and through him with God. Thus Paul depicts for us in his farewell address the entire richness of Christianity, in order to give us confidence and support for the time when he will no longer be with his Church.

The Apostle kneels down and prays " with them all." A moving picture. It has nothing to do with sentimental feeling, even though the loud weeping of his listeners must have touched him to the depths. Paul knows of the power and consolation of prayer. In his letters we can see how he is continually telling them he is praying for them. And he asks them to pray for him. In the letter to the Ephesians (6:18) we read: " Pray at all times in the Spirit, with all prayer and supplication. To that end keep alert with all perseverance, making supplication for all the saints, and also for me, that utterance may be given me in opening my mouth boldly to proclaim the mystery of the gospel." If we leave this moving description of the happenings at Miletus with such thoughts in mind, we may go on to ask ourselves whether we understand, like Paul, the meaning and obligations of being a Christian, and realize that our place among the people of God is through the mystery of the Body of Christ.

To Jerusalem by Way of Caesarea (21:1–14)

¹And when we had parted from them and set sail, we came by a straight course to Cos, and the next day to Rhodes, and from there to Patara. ²And having found a ship crossing to Phoenicia, we went aboard, and set sail. ³When we had come in sight of Cyprus, leaving it on the left we sailed to Syria, and landed at Tyre; for there the ship was to unload its cargo. ⁴And having sought out the disciples, we stayed there for seven days. Through the Spirit they told Paul not to go on to Jerusalem. ⁵And when our days there were ended, we departed and went on our journey; and they all, with wives and children, brought us on our way till we were outside the city; and kneeling down on the beach we prayed and bade one another farewell. ⁶Then we went on board the ship, and they returned home.

This passage does not require much explanation. What impresses us in it is the exactitude with which Luke has noted down the separate stages of their journey. It is clear that these are personal notes which were made during the journey itself. This sort of detailed account fills us with every confidence, even when the writer himself is not an eye-witness. The travelers change ship at Patara. Other, perhaps more reliable sources, put this change of ship further to the East, at Myrna, on the southern coast of Asia Minor. Presumably the journey across open sea required a more solid ship.

In Tyre Paul used the interruption in the journey to visit the church established there. We know nothing about its beginning. But we should not be wrong in assuming that it was founded when the Greek Jews who had become Christians were forced to flee from Jerusalem. For we are told in 11 : 19 that " those who were scattered . . . traveled as far as Phoenicia." And on their way from Antioch to the Council of the Apostles at Jerusalem, Paul and Barnabas passed through Phoenicia, " reporting the conversion of the Gentiles, and they gave great joy to all the brethren " (15 : 3). So Paul was no stranger as he " sought out the disciples " at Tyre and stayed there " for seven days." He will have assembled with the church as he did at Troas (20 : 6ff.) for the breaking of bread, for he valued every occasion and opportunity for carrying out his task as an apostle. It must have been at one of those assemblies that prophetically gifted disciples foretold the difficulties that would befall him at Jerusalem, and tried to dissuade him from going there. Paul's attitude to this can be seen in the description of a similar occasion (21 : 11ff.). The farewell at Tyre, like that at Miletus, was made painful and moving precisely in the foreknowledge of what was to come. We are told that they all, " with wives and children," knelt down on the beach and prayed. We get a very clear picture from this of the close ties existing between the members of the young church, living as they did in a hostile and rejecting environment. How moving is the respect and veneration given to the man who cares for all his " children " like a father and a mother. He tells them he is " in travail until Christ be formed in you " (Gal. 4 : 19). And the trust and helplessness of the community is expressed in the fact that they kneel down together on the ground and pray with the departing Apostle. What should we think of such a scene today? Are we prepared, inwardly and outwardly, to do likewise? Or would our greater sophistication and our present-day theology forbid it?

⁷*When we had finished the voyage from Tyre, we arrived at Ptolemais; and we greeted the brethren and stayed with them*

*for one day. ⁸On the morrow we departed and came to Caesarea;
and we entered the house of Philip the evangelist, who was one
of the seven, and stayed with him. ⁹And he had four unmarried
daughters, who phophesied. ¹⁰While we were staying for some
days, a prophet named Agabus came down from Judea. ¹¹And
coming to us he took Paul's girdle and bound his own feet and
hands, and said, " Thus says the Holy Spirit, ' So shall the Jews
at Jerusalem bind the man who owns this girdle and deliver him
into the hands of the Gentiles.' " ¹²When we heard this, we and
the people there begged him not to go up to Jerusalem. ¹³Then
Paul answered, " What are you doing, weeping and breaking
my heart? For I am ready not only to be imprisoned but even
to die at Jerusalem for the name of the Lord Jesus." ¹⁴And when
he would not be persuaded, we ceased and said, " The will of
the Lord be done."*

Caesarea becomes a special stopping place. We meet a figure
there who is familiar to us from the accounts about the work of
the " Seven " who were appointed by the apostles as their assis-
tants at the beginning of the Church's existence (chapters 6–8).
Next to Stephen we know most about Philip. We are told of the
extraordinary marks of God's favor that accompanied his work
in Samaria and of the well-known baptism of the Ethiopian
(8: 3–40). And in the last sentence we read that Philip " preached
the gospel to all the towns till he came to Caesarea." He is called
" evangelist." The word is still used in its original meaning of
preacher and messenger of salvation, not yet of writer of a
written gospel, as it came to be used later. " Evangelists " in
this original sense is used in Eph. 4: 11, side by side with
" apostles," " prophets," " pastors " and " teachers." " Do the
work of an evangelist," Timothy is told in 2 Tim. 4: 5.
    Paul and Philip—are these two men meeting here for the
first time since the days of Stephen? Then Saul had been a

" young man," one of the bitterest enemies of the Seven, and had played a special part in the stoning of Stephen, " breathing threats and murder against the disciples of the Lord " (9 : 1). The Greek convert Jews were forced to flee from Jerusalem as a result of his persecution. For the Church this was the occasion of new missionary activity. For Saul/Paul it was the way in which the Lord threw him down to the ground in order to raise him up again as his special vessel. The two men may have been thinking of all this as Paul entered the house of Philip. They had now become brothers in Christ, preachers and " evangelists."

We are told of " four daughters " of Philip. They were unmarried and possessed the gift of prophecy. We must look on them as having been consecrated to God. They bring to reality what Paul says in 1 Cor. 7 : 34 : " The unmarried woman or girl is anxious about the affairs of the Lord, how to be holy in body and spirit." There seems to be an inner connection between their virginal state of consecration to God, and their prophetic gift. We think of the prophetess Anna (Luke 2 : 36ff.) of whom we are told that after a brief marriage she lived " as a widow till she was eighty-four . . . worshiping with fasting and prayer night and day." Celibacy and spiritual vocation bear a special relationship to one another, as we can also see from the saying of the Lord : " There are eunuchs who have made themselves eunuchs for the sake of the kingdom of heaven " (Mt. 19 : 12). And we know from Paul that in the primitive Church women were active in prophecy and even in the church assemblies : " Any woman who prays or prophesies with her head unveiled dishonors her head " (1 Cor. 11 : 5).

Philip's house seems to have been a meeting place for those who had charismatic gifts. The prophet Agabus arrives from Judea and with a symbolic gesture foretells the fate threatening the Apostle in Jerusalem. In 11 : 27 we have already been told of his prophetic gift—at that time he was at Antioch. It is possible that this time he has come to meet the Apostle at Caesarea in order to point the danger out to him. That would have indicated the extent of the danger at Jerusalem and made comprehensible Paul's letter to the Romans, which he wrote in anticipation of this danger: " I appeal to you, brethren . . . to strive together with me in your prayers to God on my behalf, that I may be delivered from the unbelievers in Judea, and that my service for Jerusalem may be acceptable to the saints " (Rom. 15 : 30f.).

Paul goes to Jerusalem in the knowledge that " imprisonment and afflictions " (20 : 23) await him—following in the steps of his once suffering Lord, paying no heed to the prophetic voices, no heed to the pressing pleas of his companions and friends, in complete readiness " not only to be imprisoned but even to die at Jerusalem for the name of the Lord Jesus." Luke who accompanies him at this hour, gives us a moving description of this true disciple of Jesus, about whom the risen Lord spoke thus in Damascus: " I will show him how much he must suffer for the sake of my name " (9 : 16). We are reminded of Gethsemane when all those assembled spoke, echoing Jesus' words: " The will of the Lord be done."

Paul Is Taken Prisoner in Jerusalem and Held for Examination (21 : 15—23 : 22)

James' Advice; Paul Goes into the Temple (21 : 15-26)

[15]*After these days we made ready and went up to Jerusalem.* [16]*And some of the disciples from Caesarea went with us, bringing us to the house of Mnason of Cyprus, an early disciple, with whom we should lodge.*

[17]*When we had come to Jerusalem, the brethren received us gladly.* [18]*On the following day Paul went in with us to James;*

and all the elders were present. ¹⁹After greeting them, he related one by one the things that God had done among the Gentiles through his ministry. ²⁰And when they heard it, they glorified God. And they said to him, "You see, brother, how many thousands there are among the Jews of those who have believed; they are all zealous for the law, ²¹and they have been told about you that you teach all the Jews who are among the Gentiles to forsake Moses, telling them not to circumcise their children or observe the customs. ²²What then is to be done? They will certainly hear that you have come. ²³Do therefore what we tell you. We have four men who are under a vow; ²⁴take these men and purify yourself along with them and pay their expenses, so that they may shave their heads. Thus all will know that there is nothing in what they have been told about you but that you yourself live in observance of the law. ²⁵But as for the Gentiles who have believed, we have sent a letter with our judgment that they should abstain from what has been sacrificed to idols and from blood and from what is strangled and from unchastity." ²⁶Then Paul took the men, and the next day he purified himself with them and went into the temple, to give notice when the days of purification would be fulfilled and the offering presented for every one of them.

The entire account about Paul (from 13:1 to 28:31) can be divided into two almost equal parts, of which the first (13:1—21:14) describes Paul's great missionary work, and the second (21:15—28:31) the details of his sufferings, that is, his imprisonment. If one counts 21:1-14 as belonging to this second part, which is already overshadowed by his sufferings, then the equal length of the two parts becomes even more obvious. Was it Luke's deliberate intention in constructing these two parts of Acts to remind us of the way the gospel too is divided into Jesus' public life, and his passion?

Paul and his companions enter Jerusalem. They have gone the 75 miles or so distance on foot, or perhaps they rode on animals provided by their friends in Caesarea. The house of Mnason is not actually between Caesarea and Jerusalem but in Jerusalem itself, even though this is not clear from the text. We are told that the " brethren " received them " gladly." This no doubt refers first and foremost to the friendly welcome they received from Mnason, who was one of the earliest Greek Jewish converts.

The meeting with James was not so happy. James, the " Lord's brother " (Gal. 1 : 19), was in charge of the church at Jerusalem after Peter's departure (12 : 17). According to all we are told, he was still very much bound up with the Jewish law, even as a Christian. Thus for the conservative element among the Jewish converts to Christianity, he was a standing example and symbol of the continued existence of the old Jewish religious order. We have noted his views at the Council of the Apostles (15 : 13–21). Although he approved in principle of the freedom of the Gentile Christians from the Mosaic law, he tried nevertheless to take account of Jewish feeling with certain qualifications and prohibitions which bear his name. This same attitude is evident now too. He and the elders did indeed " glorify " God for " the things that God had done among the Gentiles " through Paul's ministry, but already we hear him expressing great anxiety when he recalls the opposition that is felt in Jewish Christian circles, let alone among Jews who are not Christians, towards the Apostle to the Gentiles. If we assume that the feast of Pentecost for which Paul, according to 20 : 16, wanted to be in Jerusalem was in fact celebrated at that time, then we can understand James' anxiety still more easily. He knows how Paul is thought of by the Jews. We are not told that he shared their criticism. His task is to ease the situation. He suggests a public act. Paul is to prove his loyalty to the law, and the error of those who accuse him.

Did Paul accept the suggestion easily? We know that he did not compromise in the question of freedom from the law. We think of the Council of the Apostles (chapter 15) and more particularly of what he says in Gal. 2:1–10. He would certainly not have moved from this position. But in the passage concerning Timothy's circumcision (16:1ff.) we saw already how Paul was able at any given time to take appropriate action to avoid difficulties, despite his principle about freedom from the law. Again we are reminded of his words in 1 Cor. 9:19–23: "For though I am free from all men, I have made myself a slave to all, that I might win the more. To the Jews I became as a Jew, in order to win Jews; to those under the law I became as one under the law—though not being myself under the law—that I might win those under the law . . . I have become all things to all men, that I might by all means save some."

We can point to the fact that once already Paul had put himself under such a vow. In 18:18 we read that "at Cenchreae he cut his hair, for he had a vow." In the light of this, the ever-wise James did not suggest anything intrinsically impossible when he advised Paul to join the "four men" who had taken a vow and "purify" himself along with them and "pay" the expenses for their purification. If Paul were to do this, then he would be showing that stubborn fanaticism, in whatever direction, was not in the spirit of the gospel and that enthusiasm must be tempered by proper consideration and concern· for others.

The Jews Rise Up against Paul; He Is Taken into Protective Custody by the Roman Overlords (21:27–39)

[27] *When the seven days were almost completed, the Jews from Asia, who had seen him in the temple, stirred up all the crowd, and laid hands on him,* [28] *crying out, "Men of Israel, help!*

This is the man who is teaching men everywhere against the people and the law and this place; moreover he also brought Greeks into the temple, and he has defiled this holy place." ²⁹*For they had previously seen Trophimus the Ephesian with him in the city, and they supposed that Paul had brought him into the temple.* ³⁰*Then all the city was aroused, and the people ran together; they seized Paul and dragged him out of the temple; and at once the gates were shut.* ³¹*And as they were trying to kill him word came to the tribune of the cohort that all Jerusalem was in confusion.* ³²*He at once took soldiers and centurions, and ran down to them; and when they saw the tribune and the soldiers, they stopped beating Paul.* ³³*Then the tribune came up and arrested him, and ordered him to be bound with two chains. He inquired who he was and what he had done.* ³⁴*Some in the crowd shouted one thing, some another; and as he could not learn the facts because of the uproar, he ordered him to be brought into the barracks.* ³⁵*And when he came to the steps, he was actually carried by the soldiers because of the violence of the crowd;* ³⁶*for the mob of the people followed, crying, "Away with him!"*

³⁷*As Paul was about to be brought into the barracks, he said to the tribune, "May I say something to you?" And he said, "Do you know Greek?* ³⁸*Are you not the Egyptian, then, who recently stirred up a revolt and led the four thousand men of the Assassins out into the wilderness?"* ³⁹*Paul replied, "I am a Jew, from Tarsus in Cilicia, a citizen of no mean city; I beg you, let me speak to the people."*

The sacrifice Paul made, externally and internally, by taking over responsibility for the purification of the four men, was in vain. The Jews of the diaspora, in their blind hatred and fanaticism, thought they saw an opportunity in Jerusalem itself and its temple to seize hold of Paul who had been difficult to capture on non-Palestinian ground. Acts vividly describes their attempts, during the Apostle's missionary travels.

It was the " Jews from Asia," that is from the region of Ephesus, who " had seen him in the temple." They seem to have come to Jerusalem for the feast of Pentecost. We recall the hostile attitude of the Jews of Ephesus (19:9) and what Paul said to the elders of the church there about the " trials " which befell him through their " plots " (20:19).

It was easy enough to lay hands on Paul among the crowd of pilgrims, and in the presence of Jews who were passionately excited about their orthodoxy, to charge him with defiling the temple. We know how strictly the Jews closed their temple to non-Jews. Warning notices marked the dividing line between the inner temple and the outer space reserved for Gentiles. On them were written these words: " Non-Jews may not cross the barrier and terrace around the temple. If anyone is caught doing so, he will be responsible for the consequences, namely, death." Flavius Josephus, the Jewish historian, refers to this regulation which was agreed to by the Roman authorities. And the Museum at Istanbul possesses one of these notices, recovered during excavations.

If Paul had really brought the Gentile Christian Trophimus from Ephesus (20:5) into the inner temple, this would, according to Jewish law, have been equivalent to defiling the temple. But the text deliberately says that they " supposed " he had been in the temple, because they had seen him in Paul's company that night. The accusation of defiling the temple was doubtless only an excuse to act against the man who was " teaching men everywhere against the people and the law and this place." In the last resort it was a blow struck by fanatical Jewish orthodoxy against the Church which was liberating herself from the Jewish law, whose most determined protagonist was Paul.

The accusation levelled against Paul at that moment may have reminded him of the time when, as a passionate enemy of the young Church, he was among those who had levelled the same accusations against Stephen that were now directed against himself. At that time it was also Jews of the diaspora, among them men " from Cilicia and Asia," of whom it was said in 6: 12ff.: " They stirred up the people and the elders and the scribes, and they came upon him and seized him and brought him before the council, and set up false witnesses who said, ' This man never ceases to speak words against this holy place and the law; for we have heard him say that this Jesus of Nazareth will destroy this place and will change the customs which Moses delivered to us.' "

The comparison surprises us. It is a most moving example of the transformation that has occurred in Saul/Paul. We are reminded of what he says in his letter to the Philippians (3: 7ff.): " I count everything as loss because of the surpassing worth of knowing Christ Jesus my Lord. For his sake I have suffered the loss of all things, and count them as refuse, in order that I may gain Christ . . . that I may know him and the power of his resurrection, and may share his sufferings, becoming like him in his death, that if possible I may attain the resurrection from the dead."

This share in his sufferings which Paul had already been experiencing, was now turned to reality in the fullest sense. For several years a victim of persecution, he is about to undergo the suffering of being a prisoner. We do not know whether he was ever again able to free himself from the hands that laid hold of him in the uproar and became for him the hands of Jesus. He is seized in the tumult that filled the whole of Jerusalem, dragged out of the temple and given over to the excited crowd. If the Roman garrison that was stationed in the temple fortress of Antonia and was ready to move at an instant's notice on the days of Jewish festivals, had not intervened, Paul would have been done to death. Luke gives us a lively and presumably eye-witness account of the way he was taken prisoner by the Romans. The Roman tribune believed he had secured a rebel leader. For the Jewish underground was forever starting movements of liberation against the Roman occupation. 5:36 already speaks of people of this sort. And the chronicles of Flavius Josephus confirm the revolt of the " Egyptian " and the four thousand " Assassins " mentioned in the text, though from a different point of view.

We note Luke's description of the " tribune " whose name, we are told in 23:26, was Claudius Lysias, as a correct and sympathetic representative of the Roman power. We shall several times later hear about his interventions on Paul's behalf. As we have repeatedly indicated, it was the aim of Acts to represent the attitude of the Roman authorities towards Paul in so friendly a light that this attitude itself becomes a favorable judgment on their prisoner. We note, moreover, that Paul tells the tribune politely but firmly about himself and his birth in the well-known town of Tarsus, in order to obtain for himself permission to address the crowd.

His Defense to the Jews (21:40—22:21)

⁴⁰*And when he had given him leave, Paul, standing on the steps, motioned with his hands to the people; and when there was a great hush, he spoke to them in the Hebrew language, saying :*

¹*" Brethren and fathers, hear the defence which I now make before you."*

²*And when they heard that he addressed them in the Hebrew language, they were the more quiet. And he said :*

³*" I am a Jew, born at Tarsus in Cilicia, but brought up in this city at the feet of Gamaliel, educated according to the strict*

*manner of the law of our fathers, being zealous for God as you
all are this day.* ⁴*I persecuted this Way to the death, binding
and delivering to prison both men and women,* ⁵*as the high
priest and the whole council of elders bear me witness. From them
I received letters to the brethren, and I journeyed to Damascus
to take those also who were there and bring them in bonds to
Jerusalem to be punished.*

⁶*And I made my journey and drew near to Damascus, about
noon a great light from heaven suddenly shone about me.* ⁷*And
I fell to the ground and heard a voice saying to me ' Saul, Saul,
why do you persecute me?'* ⁸*And I answered, ' Who are you,
Lord?' And he said to me, ' I am Jesus of Nazareth whom you
are persecuting.'* ⁹*Now those who were with me saw the light
but did not hear the voice of the one who was speaking to me.*
¹⁰*And I said, ' What shall I do, Lord?' And the Lord said to
me, ' Rise, and go into Damascus, and there you will be told
all that is appointed for you to do.'* ¹¹*And when I could not see
because of the brightness of that light, I was led by the hand
by those who were with me, and came into Damascus.*

¹²*And one Ananias, a devout man according to the law,
well spoken of by all the Jews who lived there,* ¹³*came to me,
and standing by me said to me, ' Brother Saul, receive your
sight.' And in that very hour I received my sight and saw him.*
¹⁴*And he said, ' The God of our fathers appointed you to know
his will, to see the Just One and to hear a voice from his mouth;*
¹⁵*for you will be a witness for him to all men of what you have
seen and heard.* ¹⁶*And now why do you wait? Rise and be baptized, and wash away your sins, calling on his name.'*

¹⁷*When I had returned to Jerusalem and was praying in
the temple, I fell into a trance* ¹⁸*and saw him saying to me,
' Make haste and get quickly out of Jerusalem, because they
will not accept your testimony about me.'* ¹⁹*And I said, ' Lord,
they themselves know that in every synagogue I imprisoned*

and beat those who believed in thee. [20]*And when the blood of
Stephen thy witness was shed, I also was standing by and
approving, and keeping the garments of those who killed him.'*
[21]*And he said to me, ' Depart; for I will send you far away to
the Gentiles.' "*

People have found it surprising that the Roman tribune gave
the prisoner permission to speak, and still more surprising that
those who had previously been so furious against Paul now
listened to him quietly—if only for a time. This leads us to suppose that, for literary reasons, Luke must have inserted at this
turning point in Paul's career a speech composed by himself, in
which he once again places before the readers' eyes the way Paul
has to go and the source of his message. We certainly cannot
deny Luke's part in the shaping of the speech. It can be clearly
seen from a comparison of the form and content of the three
separate accounts of Paul's calling (9: 1–30; 22:4–21; 26:9–21)
which resemble each other closely. Nevertheless it is not impossible that Paul really did make a speech in the situation that has
just been described to us, even though literary considerations
dictated the form in which the speech was written down. After
all, Luke was Paul's companion and was therefore able to share
in the experience of these things.

It is a moving account. Paul, surrounded and protected by
Roman soldiers, their commander at his side, stands on the
steps of the barracks, and makes a sign to the Jews crowding
around him, indicating that it is his intention to speak. Behind
him, a symbol of Roman power, stands the fortress built by
Herod the Great, and named " Antonia " in honor of the
Roman triumvir Mark Antony. And before him is the mighty
temple of the Jews which he still honored as the temple of his
people, even though he knew that on account of the stubborn-
ness of the Jewish leaders, it would never become the temple

of the new people of God. Paul, a native of Tarsus, was Greek-speaking. But here he deliberately uses the colloquial Hebrew language Aramaic, and it may have been this which induced the people to listen to him.

He begins his speech with a moving admission—that of his own Jewish origin. He tells them of his boyhood in Jerusalem and his teachers, among whom he cleverly gives first place to the revered Gamaliel, a man who had already made an important statement during the trial of the Apostles (5:34ff.). He speaks of his zealousness for God's law, which drove him to violent persecution of the Church and as a consequence to take the memorable path to Damascus. Again we are told of what Acts had already described in detail in 9:1–30. If the events in Damascus are recounted to us in detail yet again, and later, in 26:9–21, for a third time, this is not only to give a vivid description of Paul's current situation but to make the reader aware once more of the way he came by his great task and the importance of his calling for the future of the Church.

We shall not take exception to the small differences which are apparent if we compare the three accounts but shall try to understand the essential aspects of this incomparable story. Luke's free, untrammeled style did not concern itself with irrelevancies. This can be seen, for example, in the different ways in which the attitude of Paul's companions is described. In 9:7 we read: "The men who were traveling with him stood speechless, hearing the voice but seeing no one." In our present text it says: "Those who were with me saw the light but did not hear the voice of the one who was speaking to me." It is possible to harmonize the two accounts to some extent but this is not absolutely necessary since both stories sufficiently stress the effect on Paul's companions of these mysterious and incomprehensible events.

Again, as in 9:4 and also in 26:14, the story begins with the

question: " Saul, Saul, why do you persecute me? " The words
are identical in all three accounts. It is as though Paul heard the
echo of these words for the rest of his life. The name used,
" Saul," is evidence, even in the Greek translation, that the Lord
spoke to his persecutor " in the Hebrew language " (26:14).
And again, as in 9:8, the man who "could not see because of
the brightness of that light " let himself be led by the hand to
Damascus in order to be given back his sight by Ananias. What
is meant is internal vision, even more than external. There is
deliberate reference to the meaning of the call in Ananias's
words, which differ here from those in 9:10ff. There is mention of the " God of our fathers " and of the " Just One." Paul
was foreordained to " hear a voice from his mouth " and to
" be a witness for him to all men." The name " Jesus " and
" Christ " is at first not used, out of consideration for his
Jewish hearers. We note that the words used are exclusively
within the context of Jewish concepts regarding belief in God
and expectation of salvation. A comparison with Gal. 1:15 will
show how greatly this passage reflects true Pauline thought:
" When he who had set me apart before I was born, and had
called me through his grace, was pleased to reveal his Son to
me, in order that I might preach him among the Gentiles . . ."

The sentences that follow are not found in the other two
passages. Paul speaks of a vision in the temple when he
" returned to Jerusalem." Everything points to this having happened in the course of the first visit he made to Jerusalem after
he had received his special calling from Christ. 9:26ff. and
Gal. 1:18 tell us something about this. There too we are told
that he only remained a short time in Jerusalem. But of the
extraordinary encounter with the Lord we read only here.

Why does Paul speak of it? He is taking account of the feelings of the Jews. That he was " praying in the temple " was a
sign that even as a Christian he remained faithful to the Jewish

holy of holies and did not, as he was accused of doing, defile the temple. And it was precisely here, in this temple, that the Lord spoke with him. He is referring to the Risen Lord. But the words as they stand can refer to the Lord God of the Old Testament in the Jewish sense. It was vital for the Apostle at this time to be able to attribute his mission and calling to the authority of God—the same God whom the Jews also worshiped.

And if Paul's speech reminded his listeners of the time when he himself pursued the Christians from one synagogue to the next and actually participated in the stoning of Stephen, this was once again done deliberately as a way of appealing to their own beliefs. For it would have made them realize that it was not disloyalty towards the temple and the Jewish way of life that turned him into a Christian and a disciple of Jesus, but, on the contrary, obedience to God's call.

He Is in Danger of Being Scourged (22 : 22–29)

²²Up to this word they listened to him; then they lifted up their voices and said, " Away with such a fellow from the earth! For he ought not to live." ²³And as they cried out and waved their garments and threw dust into the air, ²⁴the tribune commanded him to be brought into the barracks, and ordered him to be examined by scourging, to find out why they shouted thus against him. ²⁵But when they had tied him up with the thongs, Paul said to the centurion who was standing by, " Is it lawful for you to scourge a man who is a Roman citizen, and uncondemned? " ²⁶When the centurion heard that, he went to the tribune and said to him, " What are you about to do? For this man is a Roman citizen." ²⁷So the tribune came and said to him, " Tell me, are you a Roman citizen? " And he said,

" Yes." ²⁸The tribune answered, " I bought this citizenship for a large sum." Paul said, " But I was born a citizen." ²⁹So those who were about to examine him withdrew from him instantly; and the tribune also was afraid, for he realized that Paul was a Roman citizen and that he had bound him.

As has already happened on several occasions in Acts (7:54; 17:32), the speaker is interrupted in the course of his speech. The chief reason seems to have been the statement about the mission to the Gentiles, which once again passionately aroused the fanaticism of the Jews. It is true, of course, that they themselves engaged in missionary activity among other peoples. But only in order to convert them to the Mosaic law. We remember Jesus' severe judgment in Matthew 23:15: " Woe to you, scribes and Pharisees, hypocrites! for you traverse sea and land to make a single proselyte, and when he becomes a proselyte, you make him twice as much a child of hell as yourselves."

The Jews knew only too well what the message was that Paul brought to the Gentiles. They knew, as is shown in 21:28, what his attitude was to the law and to circumcision; they knew about his contradiction of the Jewish teaching about salvation. And in their slavishly rigid adherence to tradition, they were appalled at his temerity in suggesting that his mission was at the command of God. We do not need logic or much psychology to explain their attitude. In the presence of fanaticism, rational evidence, especially in the religious sphere, counts for nothing.

Can we really blame the Roman tribune who up to now had behaved correctly and justly, for beginning to feel uneasy vis-à-vis the turbulent crowd, and to believe himself obliged to examine Paul by the painful method of scourging? It was precisely this that gave Paul the opportunity to invoke the Roman citizenship that had been his from birth. The intention of Acts is to show that Paul was under the protection of the Holy Spirit and at the same time to describe the correct attitude of the Roman tribune, who desisted from the scourging as soon as the position had been explained to him.

Before the Chief Priests and the Council (22:30—23:11)

³⁰*But on the morrow, desiring to know the real reason why the Jews accused him, he unbound him, and commanded the chief priests and all the council to meet, and he brought Paul down and set him before them.*

¹*And Paul looking intently at the council, said, "Brethren, I have lived before God in all good conscience up to this day."* ²*And the high priest Ananias commanded those who stood by him to strike him on the mouth.* ³*Then Paul said to him, "God shall strike you, you whitewashed wall! Are you sitting to judge me according to the law, and yet contrary to the law you order me to be struck?"* ⁴*Those who stood by said, "Would you revile God's high priest?"* ⁵*And Paul said, "I did not know, brethren, that he was the high priest; for it is written, 'You shall not speak evil of a ruler of your people.'"*

⁶*But when Paul perceived that one part were Sadducees and the other Pharisees, he cried out in the council, "Brethren, I am a Pharisee, a son of Pharisees; with respect to the hope and the resurrection of the dead I am on trial."* ⁷*And when he had said this, a dissension arose between the Pharisees and the Sadducees; and the assembly was divided.* ⁸*For the Sadducees say that there is no resurrection, nor angel, nor spirit; but the Pharisees acknowledge them all.* ⁹*Then a great clamor arose; and some of the scribes of the Pharisees' party stood up and contended, "We find nothing wrong in this man. What if a spirit or an angel spoke to him?"* ¹⁰*And when the dissension became violent, the tribune, afraid that Paul would be torn in*

*pieces by them, commanded the soldiers to go down and take
him by force from among them and bring him into the barracks.*

*[11]The following night the Lord stood by him and said, " Take
courage, for as you have testified about me at Jerusalem, so you
must bear witness also at Rome."*

A memorable scene. Paul stands before the council. In earlier
days he had been in high favor with the Jewish authorities,
attacking the Church with their agreement and support. He even
began his activity against the Christians of Damascus with letters
from the high priest; But now he himself was their prisoner,
undergoing examination at their hands. We shall not attempt
to make any accurate assessment of the account given here. We
could indeed ask whether the details conform to the situation
as it truly was, whether in fact the Roman tribune was able to
command the presence of the council, whether he himself could
be present at its meetings and Paul proceed forthwith to make
a speech. In other words, what we are given here is not the
complete process of a legal trial, and this applies also to the later
accounts. Luke is confining himself only to essentials. If we
assume, with some justification, that he was staying in Jerusalem
near Paul, we must also assume that he was reliably informed
about Paul's affairs.

Paul brings the process to a surprising conclusion. He
acknowledges himself a Pharisee and insists that it was the
Pharisees' hope of a resurrection that had brought him to trial.
A clever tactic, so it appears to us. Was it really unworthy of
an apostle, as some would have it? Did Paul still have the right
to call himself a Pharisee? Or was he merely using the concept
to mislead his audience? He surely took it seriously. But he
used the word with a new meaning. Once he had been a
Pharisee. In his speech before Agrippa (26:5) he says :
" According to the strictest party of our religion I have lived

as a Pharisee." But he was no longer as he had been before. And yet he does not refrain from writing of himself in Phil. 3:5, à propos of the Judaizers, as "a Hebrew born of Hebrews; as to the law a Pharisee . . ." Even though this is said about the past, it is still relevant to the present.

Paul confronts the Jews in the knowledge of the tie that binds him to the Pharisees, even as a Christian. This tie is based on the "hope" of Israel and the "resurrection of the dead." Paul would certainly have given these ideas a new meaning in the light of his encounter with Christ. But in his discussion with orthodox Jewry he could employ them as a common starting point in much the same way as he had sought to find common ground with the Greeks on the Areopagus.

We have no reason, therefore, to criticize Luke's description of Paul's clever tactic. Luke makes it sound both credible and meaningful. With it comes a lively description of the tensions within Judaism, above all between Pharisees and Sadducees. We know from the gospel account that the Sadducees disputed the reality of the human spirit and the continuance of life after physical death. Flavius Josephus confirms this also. The Sadducees' denial of the existence of pure spirits belongs to the same category, though we have no extra-biblical evidence for it. The existence of spiritual beings, generally called angels, is part of the continuous teaching of the New Testament. With all the differences in concept, the belief of pious Jews thus continues to live on in the Church.

The divisive word has been said. The two parties begin violently to disagree. The Pharisees are on Paul's side. Their hatred of the Sadducees was at that moment stronger than their dislike of the Apostle. The soldiers take Paul back to the barracks. The tribune saves his life. The entire scene is recreated in the tribune's letter to the governor Felix where he writes (23:28f.): "Desiring to know the charge on which they accused him, I brought him down to their council. I found that he was accused about questions of their law, but charged with nothing deserving death or imprisonment."

We hear this again and again during the other stages of Paul's trial. Luke makes a point of stressing the verdict of the Roman judges. But their efforts seem hopeless. Paul's Jewish accusers remain unreconciled and show themselves prepared to use every means at their disposal to secure a conviction. And so the situation remains until the appeal to the Emperor.

Did Paul really intend to sow dissension among the council by the statement that he was a Pharisee? We cannot be certain of his real intention. He was concerned above all to win over the Pharisees. But at the end he seems to have been very troubled and anxious about the situation as he was taken into captivity. Luke has good reason for putting the account of the Lord's night appearance at this point in his story. The Lord's words sound like a prophecy of Paul's rescue from the Jews: " Take courage, for as you have testified about me at Jerusalem, so you must bear witness also at Rome." We are reminded of 19:21 where Paul said: "After I have been there [at Jerusalem], I must also see Rome."

The Jews Plot to Kill Him (23:12-22)

¹²*When it was day, the Jews made a plot and bound themselves by an oath neither to eat nor drink till they had killed Paul.* ¹³*There were more than forty who made this conspiracy.* ¹⁴*And they went to the chief priests and elders, and said, " We have strictly bound ourselves by an oath to taste no food till we have killed Paul.* ¹⁵*You therefore, along with the council, give notice now to the tribune to bring him down to you, as though you were going to determine his case more exactly. And we are ready to kill him before he comes near."*

16Now the son of Paul's sister heard of their ambush; so he went and entered the barracks and told Paul. 17And Paul called one of the centurions and said, " Bring this young man to the tribune; for he has something to tell him." 18So he took him and brought him to the tribune and said, " Paul the prisoner called me and asked me to bring this young man to you, as he has something to say to you." 19The tribune took him by the hand, and going aside asked him privately, " What is that you have to tell me?" 20And he said, " The Jews have agreed to ask you to bring Paul down to the council tomorrow, as though they were going to inquire somewhat more closely about him. 21But do not yield to them; for more than forty of their men lie in ambush for him, having bound themselves by an oath neither to eat nor drink till they have killed him; and now they are ready, waiting for the promise from you." 22So the tribune dismissed the young man, charging him, " Tell no one that you have informed me of this."

This passage describes the hopelessness of Paul's situation in Jerusalem, and the fanatical hatred the Jews bore him. It also shows how, in the time of his greatest need, he was helped most immediately and effectively by him who, in the vision at night, urged him to take courage and have trust. Paul's situation was in truth dangerous. The conspirators who had bound themselves by the strictest possible oath to destroy Paul, presumably reckoned on the tribune bringing him with only a token guard for interrogation by the council. It had been so at the previous hearing. The tribune asked for military support only when the two Jewish factions began to dispute among themselves. The very great danger to the Apostle's life is shown by the fact that the conspirators were able to include their leaders in the plot.

But again the power of the Lord watching over his messengers is clearly revealed. Acts often astonishes us by what it has to tell of the concrete ways which the Lord uses to serve his purposes. We have an example here in the intervention of the nephew who otherwise takes no part in the story. The Spirit watching over Paul guides the young man to the barracks. How did he learn of the plot? It is possible that a member of the council, one of the group of Pharisees who were well disposed towards Paul, alerted Paul's sister to the danger. We can only go on guessing. Many possibilities are open to God.

Again we compare the attitude of the Jews with that of the Roman tribune. The Roman authorities are shown to be both well-intentioned and objective when they permit the young man to see the prisoner and to speak with the officer in charge who received him readily and took seriously what he had to say. The wisdom and prudence of the tribune is revealed at the same time. He told the young man to keep quiet about the information he had brought, so that a premature alarm would not bring more danger for Paul. The tribune planned to take the prisoner to a safer place during the darkness of the night.

In Caesarea (23:23—26:32)

He Is Taken to Caesarea by Roman Soldiers (23:23–35)

[23]*Then he called two of the centurions and said, " At the third hour of the night get ready two hundred soldiers with seventy horsemen and two hundred spearmen to go as far as Caesarea.* [24]*Also provide mounts for Paul to ride, and bring him safely to Felix the governor."* [25]*And he wrote a letter to this effect :*

[26]*" Claudius Lysias to his Excellency the governor Felix, greeting.* [27]*This man was seized by the Jews, and was about to be*

killed by them, when I came upon them with the soldiers and rescued him, having learned that he was a Roman citizen. [28]And desiring to know the charge on which they accused him, I brought him down to their council. [29]I found that he was accused about questions of their law, but charged with nothing deserving death or imprisonment. [30]And when it was disclosed to me that there would be a plot against the man, I sent him to you at once, ordering his accusers also to state before you what they have against him."

[31]*So the soldiers, according to their instructions, took Paul and brought him by night to Antipatris. [32]And on the morrow they returned to the barracks, leaving the horsemen to go on with him. [33]When they came to Caesarea and delivered the letter to the governor, they presented Paul also before him. [34]On reading the letter, he asked to what province he belonged. When he learned that he was from Cilicia [35]he said, " I will hear you when your accusers arrive." And he commanded him to be guarded in Herod's praetorium.*

The tribune took the young man's warning seriously. The books of Flavius Josephus tell us of the various uprisings on the part of the Jewish underground movement against the Roman occupation. Thus we can understand why the tribune alerted so large a troop of soldiers to accompany the prisoner safely to Caesarea during the night, and to deliver him into the immediate charge of the governor himself. It would have been worse than merely awkward for the tribune if Paul, the Roman citizen, had lost his life in Jerusalem or on the way to Caesarea in a Jewish ambush. It is possible, too, that personal sympathy for Paul or dislike of the Jews played its part in his action. In the last resort, of course, here as elsewhere, it is the intention of Acts to show that there is One on high who is guiding and watching over Paul's path.

The letter which the tribune writes to his superior is evidence both of professional skill and of concern for the prisoner. We cannot really object to his describing the circumstances of the imprisonment in his own favor and making it appear that he wanted all along to protect Paul, the Roman citizen. What is important and in line with the general intention of Acts is the evidence in the letter to the effect that Paul had done nothing deserving punishment. All he had done was to direct the hostility of the Jews against himself. But they accused him only on matters concerning their own religion. We are reminded here of the judgment of the proconsul Gallio (18 : 15). The governor Festus (25 : 18f.) will be shown to have the same attitude. Everything that is said about Paul in Acts gives the impression that from the point of view of Roman law, there are no reasons to condemn him. The governor Felix too, who takes charge of Paul after the latter had been brought as prisoner to Caesarea where Felix had his seat of office, shows himself favorably disposed towards him. In 24 : 23 he specifically orders him to be given " some liberty " while in prison and to have the possibility of being cared for by his friends.

Trial Before the Governor Felix (24 : 1–27)

THE JEWS SET OUT THEIR CASE AGAINST PAUL (24 : 1–9)

[1]*And after five days the high priest Ananias came down with some elders and a spokesman, one Tertullus. They laid before the governor their case against Paul;* [2]*and when he was called, Tertullus began to accuse him, saying :*

" Since through you we enjoy much peace, and since by your provision, most excellent Felix, reforms are introduced on behalf of this nation, [3]*in every way and everywhere we accept this with*

all gratitude. [4]*But, to detain you no further, I beg you in your kindness to hear us briefly.* [5]*For we have found this man a pestilent fellow, an agitator among all the Jews throughout the world, and a ringleader of the sect of the Nazarenes.* [6]*He even tried to profane the temple, but we seized him.* [(7-)8]*By examining him yourself you will be able to learn from him about everything of which we accuse him."*

[9]*The Jews also joined in the charge, affirming that all this was so.*

The firm attitude of the Romans forces the Jews to resort to a legal trial. The decision to follow Paul to Caesarea was evidence of their determination to have Paul condemned and thus put out of harm's way by the governor. A passionately held, blind, narrow fanaticism will do anything to destroy those who oppose it! We are reminded of the Jews at Jesus' trial who did their best to force Pilate to make an adverse judgment. The situation in Caesarea can be compared to the trial before Pilate in the sense that Paul too has to go before a governor who is fairly well disposed towards him but, like Pilate, is not as uniformly convinced in his favor as, for example, the proconsul Gallio was at Corinth (18:12ff.). The words (24:26) that " he hoped that money would be given him by Paul " and the fact that he let two years go by without a clear decision and at his departure " desiring to do the Jews a favor . . . left Paul in prison " (24:27) do not speak in his favor. Nevertheless the fact that he did not hand Paul over, despite the pressure put upon him by the Jews, shows that he could find no real reason to give way to Paul's Jewish accusers.

The Jewish prosecutor cleverly manages to bring into his accusation details about the wise governorship of Felix, of which we also know independently from history. He sought to transfer the accusation against Paul on to the political plane by describing him as an " agitator among all the Jews throughout the world." Jesus too was accused in the same way. We read in Luke (23:2) that the Jews complained to Pilate: " We found this man perverting our nation, and forbidding us to give tribute to Caesar, and saying that he himself is Christ a king." The whole story repeats itself with Paul and has repeated itself ever since.

Paul is described as a " ringleader of the sect of the Nazarenes." This is indirect evidence of his reputation and his leading position in the primitive Church. The word " sect " is used in the neutral sense of group or " party " (5:17; 15:5; 26:5) but has here a definitely dismissive ring, which is increased by the prosecutor's contemptuous description of Christians as " Nazarenes." This is the only place in the New Testament where the word is used. The additional charge of profaning the temple is deliberately inserted by the prosecutor. The Romans had bound themselves to recognize the Jewish religion and to protect it. The Jews could have dealt with Paul through their own temple police as a profaner of the temple, and Tertullus cleverly makes it appear as though they seized him only on account of the profaning of the temple, and it was the Roman tribune who had deprived them of the possibility of judging him according to their law. Though the text as we have it shows some ambiguities here.

PAUL JUSTIFIES HIMSELF (24: 10–21)

[10]*And when the governor had motioned to him to speak, Paul replied :*

" Realizing that for many years you have been judge over this nation, I cheerfully make my defence. [11]*As you may ascertain, it is not more than twelve days since I went up to worship at Jerusalem;* [12]*and they did not find me disputing with any one or*

*stirring up a crowd, either in the temple or in the synagogues,
or in the city.* ¹³*Neither can they prove to you what they now
bring up against me.* ¹⁴*But this I admit to you, that according
to the Way, which they call a sect, I worship the God of our
fathers, believing everything laid down by the law or written
in the prophets,* ¹⁵*having a hope in God which these themselves
accept, that there will be a resurrection of both the just and the
unjust.* ¹⁶*So I always take pains to have a clear conscience toward
God and toward men.* ¹⁷*Now after some years I came to bring
to my nation alms and offerings.* ¹⁸*As I was doing this, they
found me purified in the temple, without any crowd or tumult.
But some Jews from Asia*—¹⁹*they ought to be here before you
and to make an accusation, if they have anything against me.*
²⁰*Or else let these men themselves say what wrongdoing they
found when I stood before the council,* ²¹*except this one thing
which I cried out while standing among them, ' With respect to
the resurrection of the dead I am on trial before you this day.' "*

Paul now pleads his own cause. He begins by expressing his
trust in Felix who had been governor from 52–60 (53–61?), and
indeed, having for " many years " been " judge," that is, in
charge of the chief administrative and legal processes, was able
to learn a great deal of the circumstances in Judea. Paul does
not make a detailed defence but only refers to the principal
accusations made against him. It need not concern us here that
the form of the speech is due to Luke's literary style. This
account, like its predecessor, is the result of personal experience
or reliable information from others.

The reason Paul gives for his visit to Jerusalem was
" worship." It was religion alone that brought him to the
temple. Even if later (verse 17) he says that he came to bring
" alms and offerings " to his people, this is merely an added
religious reason. This unambiguous reference to his motives

shows clearly that he had no other reason for coming. He firmly rejects all accusations that seek to turn him into a trouble maker and disturber of the peace.

Paul is no troublemaker in the sense of the accusation, no rebel against the existing order. Just as Jesus, rightly understood, with his teaching about the kingdom of God, disturbed men's atrophied beliefs and preconceptions and moved them to the very depths of their being, so Paul did likewise. He was perfectly aware of it: " This I admit to you, that according to the Way, which they call a sect, I worship the God of our fathers."

Paul knows that this is what really scandalizes the Jews. And he therefore tries to show that the way of salvation, which they contemptuously dismiss as a " sect," is fundamentally nothing other than the properly understood message of the " law " or the " prophets." In his speech to the Jews (in 22:14) he had already spoken of the " God of our fathers " and thereby tried to show the common basis of their belief. Now at his trial, before the leaders of the Jews, he does the same. Again he points to their joint " hope in God " and in the expectation of the resurrection of all men, " the just and the unjust," at the end of time when the promise is fulfilled.

This is a surprising rejoinder. Paul is accused of betraying the religion of the fathers and assures them that he is worshiping the " God of our fathers." He is accused of being a disturber of the peace and a troublemaker. And he replies by acknowledging a " hope in God " and the belief in the " resurrection " held in common with his accusers. His arguments are bold and challenging, and yet he is talking entirely within the context of Jesus' message. Matthew 5:17 tells us how Jesus, defending himself before his Jewish accusers, said: " Think not that I have come to abolish the law and the prophets; I have come not to abolish them but to fulfill them." He did not want to create a division between the new revelation and the old belief it was transcending. He wanted to show the gospel as the fulfillment of what had gone before. And this too was the intention of the early Church, particularly when it had to encounter the Old Jewish faith.

It is true, of course, that the relationship between the old and the new had often to express itself in a bold interpretation of the Old Testament, if it wanted to reveal an inner continuity. This is shown in the free and sometimes surprising Old Testament commentaries found in the New Testament. Paul is very aware of this, but he also knows that only where the Spirit reigns and not the letter (cf. Rom. 7:6; 2 Cor. 3:6) is it possible to find a christological interpretation in the Old Testament revelation. Where faith is able to see the work of God in Christ Jesus and to understand it in the light of the Holy Spirit, there it is both possible and permissible to look for and to find the mystery of Christ revealed in the Old Testament. But because such faith was only given to those who opened themselves to the grace of the revealing God, the Jews—as we are most movingly told in the gospels and by Paul—were prevented from seeing and understanding the relationship between gospel and Judaism, in the context of Salvation history.

Paul reminds his listeners of his interrogation by the high priest and the council, in order yet again to insist on his innocence. Or is his motive here as it was there, to separate the Pharisees from among his accusers in order to cause division once more among the Jews? Were there Pharisees present anyway? Our text (24:1) speaks only of the "high priest . . . with some elders and a spokesman." Thus he could scarcely count on the Pharisees, who had supported him on that other occasion before the council. But again he calls out quite deliberately, as he had done earlier: "With respect to the resurrection of the dead I am on trial before you this day." He is speaking here in the light of the gospel teaching but he is also referring to the belief of the Jews, in order to stress the injustice of the accusation.

POSTPONEMENT OF THE VERDICT (24: 22–27)

²²But Felix, having a rather accurate knowledge of the Way, put them off, saying " When Lysias the tribune comes down, I will decide your case." ²³Then he gave orders to the centurion that he should be kept in custody but should have some liberty, and that none of his friends should be prevented from attending to his needs.

²⁴After some days Felix came with his wife Drusilla, who was a Jewess; and he sent for Paul and heard him speak upon faith in Christ Jesus. ²⁵And as he argued about justice and self-control and future judgment, Felix was alarmed and said, " Go away for the present; when I have an opportunity I will summon you." ²⁶At the same time he hoped that money would be given him by Paul. So he sent for him often and conversed with him. ²⁷But when two years had elapsed, Felix was succeeded by Porcius Festus; and desiring to do the Jews a favor, Felix left Paul in prison.

Felix is convinced that Paul is a victim of Jewish fanaticism. He did indeed have " a rather accurate knowledge of the Way " (the Christian teaching). His third wife, Drusilla, who is mentioned here, was a Jewish princess, the daughter of Agrippa I, of whom we read in 12: 1ff., and sister of Agrippa II and Bernice, of whom we shall read in the next chapter. It may not be irrelevant to note that Felix, with the help of a magician, had made Drusilla unattractive to her husband, King Azizus of Emesa, and thus won her for himself. We can understand how he grew " alarmed," as Acts relates, when Paul told him and

Drusilla about " faith in Christ Jesus," and about " justice and self-control and future judgment." People in his situation like to avoid all serious questions and discussions. Their own life is too great a contradiction of what the evidence of preachers and ultimately also their own awakened conscience might say to them. We must hold it in Drusilla's favor that, unlike Herodias, the illegal wife of Herod Antipas, she did not seek to revenge herself on Paul and demand his death. Though in a later textual variation we note an attempt to hold her responsible for the fact that when Felix departed, he left Paul, the prisoner, to an uncertain fate.

It is not easy to judge Felix. One has the feeling that Luke is deliberately holding himself back. He knew of course about the doubtful marriage with Drusilla, but let it go without comment. When, however, he tells us that Felix hoped for a bribe or ransom money, this gives us an indication of his character but is not intended as a criticism. But the fact that Felix too saw no occasion to act against Paul in his capacity as Roman official, and even granted him " some liberty " in prison and contact with his friends, is a clear addition to the continuous evidence in Acts that no representative of Roman authority was able to find any real reason for complaint against him.

Trial before Festus; Paul Appeals to Caesar (25:1–12)

¹Now when Festus had come into his province, after three days he went up to Jerusalem from Caesarea. ²And the chief priests and the principal men of the Jews informed him against Paul; and they urged him, ³asking as a favor to have the man sent to Jerusalem, planning an ambush to kill him on the way. ⁴Festus replied that Paul was being kept at Caesarea, and that he himself intended to go there shortly. ⁵" So," said he, " let the men of

authority among you go down with me, and if there is anything wrong about the man, let them accuse him."

⁶When he had stayed among them not more than eight or ten days, he went down to Caesarea; and the next day he took his seat on the tribunal and ordered Paul to be brought. ⁷And when he had come, the Jews who had gone down from Jerusalem stood about him, bringing against him many serious charges which they could not prove. ⁸Paul said in his defense, " Neither against the law of the Jews, nor against the temple, nor against Caesar have I offended at all." ⁹But Festus, wishing to do the Jews a favor, said to Paul, " Do you wish to go up to Jerusalem, and there be tried on these charges before me? " ¹⁰But Paul said, " I am standing before Caesar's tribunal, where I ought to be tried; to the Jews I have done no wrong, as you know very well ¹¹If then I am a wrongdoer, and have committed anything for which I deserve to die, I do not seek to escape death; but if there is nothing in their charges against me, no one can give me up to them. I appeal to Caesar." ¹²Then Festus, when he had conferred with his council, answered, " You have appealed to Caesar; to Caesar you shall go."

The process against Paul is coming closer and closer to its conclusion. Felix had let the matter drag on with no clear end in sight. But his successor, Festus, seems determined to bring it to speedy close. We do not know a great deal about Festus. He is described as a conscientious, sober and clear thinking official, and as such he appears in this account.

When the Jewish leaders, and above all the " chief priests " of the Sadducees, urged Festus, the moment he visited Jerusalem for the first time, to send Paul back there, they clearly showed that their hatred of the prisoner had not grown less, even after his two years' imprisonment and interrogation. Will they try again to kill him by means of an ambush? And are they counting on the fact that the new governor is ignorant of their earlier attempts?

Festus does not grant their request. Was he aware of the situation, and of the intention of the Jews? Or was he acting with proper judiciousness by endeavoring to clarify in his own mind the circumstances of the case, and to inform himself of it fully? We incline to the latter supposition (cf. 25:16). He promises to see to the matter shortly, leaving open the question of guilt and withholding judgment. The Jewish accusers once again go to Caesarea. And again Paul is put before the representatives of the Roman law to hear their " many serious charges " against him.

What charges were these? They were nothing new. They will have been the same accusations that were made in the preceding trials. For the governor, too, they could not have been new. His " council," who are mentioned in verse 12, will have told him of the case from the documentation available and the pre-trial interrogations. Paul's reply also shows that the accusations were of long standing. These accusations were basically nothing but a pretext for their irreconcilable hatred of the man who had once belonged to their number and was now preaching to the whole world the message of him whom they had crucified. If we remember this we shall see the same motives at work in Paul's trial as there were in Jesus'.

Paul knows that argument will be useless against such passionate hatred. One has the impression that his brief reply is made only to fulfill the requirements of the law. It would have been of special interest to the Roman readers of Acts, and especially to Theophilus, to whom the book is dedicated (Luke 1:3; Acts 1:1), that Paul was able to explain without contradiction: " Neither against the law of the Jews, nor against the temple, nor against Caesar have I offended at all." These three points summarize everything that could possibly be called in question. If, as we have several times repeated, Acts was written while Paul was still on trial and written on his behalf, a sentence like the one quoted above would be especially effective.

How does the governor react? We are surprised at his offer to transfer the trial to Jerusalem and there conduct the interrogation anew, with himself as judge. What is the motive of this Roman governor? He wanted " to do the Jews a favor," we are told. A few lines later (25:18f.), the same governor says to Agrippa: " When the accusers stood up, they brought no charge in this case of such evils as I supposed; but they had certain points of dispute with him about their own superstition and about one Jesus, who was dead, but whom Paul asserted to be alive. Being at a loss how to investigate these questions, I asked whether he wished to go to Jerusalem and be tried there regarding them." One might very well ask how Festus believed he could clarify this matter better in Jerusalem. He clearly intended to make some kind of approach to the Jews.

Paul senses the danger. He will have remembered the outcome of Jesus' trial, even though at that time he himself would still have been on the side of the persecuting Jews. It is most revealing that it was this same Luke who so clearly showed in his gospel how the governor Pilate, with all his original sympathy for Jesus, and despite his conviction about Jesus' innocence, nevertheless gave in at the end: " Pilate gave sentence that their demand should be granted. He released the man who had been thrown into prison for insurrection and murder, whom they asked for; but Jesus he delivered up to their will " (Luke 23:24f.).

Paul is a Roman citizen. He puts a clear end to the uncertainties of the governor. He appeals to the justice of the emperor. He wants to be judged by him. He protests once again with a personal appeal to the governor against the accusations levelled at him by the Jews. His words are moving. He does not seek to escape punishment, should they be able to prove charges against him that require the death penalty. And he makes it sound like a criticism of the governor when he says: "But if there is nothing in their charges against me, no one can give me up to them. I appeal to Caesar." The words in which he announces his decision to a judge grown hesitant and uncertain sound clear and definite. The legal advisors of the governor give their consent to the Apostle's request. Paul is fighting for his rights. Again, as we said earlier, it is not a matter of his private life but of his standing as an Apostle, a witness of Christ, a representative of the Church.

Paul's appeal to Caesar leads him to Rome. We find it hard to understand what this means to him. As prisoner he will be going to Rome in a sense quite different from that intended by the letter to the Romans. There he wrote: "But now, since I no longer have any room for work in these regions, and since I have longed for many years to come to you, I hope to see you in passing as I go to Spain, and to be sped on my journey there by you, once I have enjoyed your company for a little." What was in Luke's mind when he wrote about the appeal to Caesar? Was Paul with him at the time in Rome, still a prisoner under interrogation, still waiting for the success of his appeal? Again we are confronted by the question of the dating of Acts, and we shall continue to be confronted by it.

Paul and Agrippa (25:13—26:32)

FESTUS TELLS AGRIPPA ABOUT PAUL (25:13-22)

[13]Now when some days had passed, Agrippa the king and Bernice arrived at Caesarea to welcome Festus. [14]And as they stayed there many days, Festus laid Paul's case before the king,

saying, " There is a man left prisoner by Felix; [15]*and when I was at Jerusalem, the chief priests and the elders of the Jews gave information about him, asking for sentence against him.* [16]*I answered them that it was not the custom of the Romans to give up anyone before the accused met the accusers face to face, and had opportunity to make his defense concerning the charge laid against him.* [17]*When therefore they came together here, I made no delay, but on the next day took my seat on the tribunal and ordered the man to be brought in.* [18]*When the accusers stood up, they brought no charge in his case of such evils as I supposed;* [19]*but they had certain points of dispute with him about their own superstition and about one Jesus, who was dead, but whom Paul asserted to be alive.* [20]*Being at a loss how to investigate these questions, I asked whether he wished to go to Jerusalem and be tried there regarding them.* [21]*But when Paul had appealed to be kept in custody for the decision of the emperor, I commanded him to be held until I could send him to Caesar."* [22]*And Agrippa said to Festus, " I should like to hear the man myself." " Tomorrow," said he " you shall hear him."*

We have here a new element in the continuously changing situation around Paul. A new figure appears. Luke deliberately uses him as witness on behalf of the Apostle. Agrippa II, son of Herod Agrippa I who had died in 44 A.D., grandson of Herod " the Great," had been entrusted by the Emperor Claudius, after he had completed his education at Rome in the year 50 with the command over areas of Syria and Palestine, and had enjoyed the favor of succeeding emperors also, including Nero, who in the year 61 A.D. made him ruler over Galilee and Perea as well. Thus the judgment of this man, who was influential in Rome, was of obvious interest to the writer of Acts in the light of his known intentions. And Agrippa's attitude would have been doubly valuable if his judgment had been able to be put at the service of the appeal in Rome. Agrippa's opinions would have been especially influential with Nero, under whom the Apostle was imprisoned in Rome.

Luke, who must have been aware of the details, is tactful in Bernice's regard, giving us her name but making no mention of the fact that she was Agrippa's sister, that after her first two marriages, they had become lovers, and that she was notorious for her loose morals. Drusilla, of whom we read in 24:24, was Bernice's sister. It is exceedingly moving to note how the imprisoned Apostle was entirely at the mercy of people of this sort and dependent on their judgment. Two differing world views here confront each other. Paul may have been struck to the heart by what he wrote in 1 Cor. 2:14: "The unspiritual man does not receive the gifts of the spirit of God, for they are folly to him, and he is not able to understand them because they are spiritually discerned. The spiritual man judges all things but is himself to be judged by no one."

There is not much to be said of what the governor Felix tells King Agrippa about Paul. Luke will have given the account its literary form. As in the letter of the tribune Lysias to the governor Felix (23:26ff.), so here too the facts are depicted in favor of the writer. But on the whole Festus' statement confirms the Roman judgment on Paul. This is shown above all in the sentence: "When the accusers stood up, they brought no charge in his case of such evils as I supposed; but they had certain points of dispute with him about their own superstition and about one Jesus, who was dead, but whom Paul asserted to be alive." Again therefore this is proof that Paul had in no way offended against Roman law, but was the victim of purely religious disagreements and of Jewish hatred. If this is the judgment of a Roman official then, together with Agrippa's own view, it could only have been in the Apostle's favor.

PAUL JUSTIFIES HIMSELF BEFORE AGRIPPA (25 : 23—26 : 23)

²³So on the morrow Agrippa and Bernice came with great pomp, and they entered the audience hall with the military tribunes and the prominent men of the city. Then by command of Festus Paul was brought in. ²⁴And Festus said, " King Agrippa and all who are present with us, you see this man about whom the whole Jewish people petitioned me, both at Jerusalem and here, shouting that he ought not to live any longer. ²⁵But I found that he had done nothing deserving death; and as he himself appealed to the emperor, I decided to send him. ²⁶But I have nothing definite to write to my lord about him. Therefore I have brought him before you, and especially before you, King Agrippa, that, after we have examined him, I may have something to write. ²⁷For it seems to me unreasonable, in sending a prisoner, not to indicate the charges against him."

Again a memorable occasion, reported by Luke. The atmosphere is strangely tense. The Roman governor, those curious siblings, Agrippa and Bernice, surrounded by a large retinue of officers and officials, full of pomp and splendor—and facing them, the prisoner. The curious, greedy eyes of sensation mongers are fixed upon him. Perhaps they regarded him with that sense of shyness which sometimes affects the worldly when confronting those who preach about another world that is closed to them.

We cannot help remembering another preacher of the gospel who faced a specially invited audience in this same town of Caesarea. The Roman centurion Cornelius, so we are told in 10 : 24ff., had invited his relations and close friends to wait for Peter, in order that they might hear all that he had been " commanded by the Lord." The two scenes curiously resemble each other. Both times men are waiting, both times their attention is fixed on an Apostle. And yet what a difference! A difference of motive and inner disposition. In their depths, of course, all the listeners are filled with the same insecurity and the same need to seek for God. But in the one case they are openly seeking and ready for salvation; in the other they react with sceptical though well-intentioned interest to the teaching of another world. Cornelius appears very different from Agrippa and Bernice. Those who are called to preach and witness to the gospel are faced again and again with such a situation.

And again we read with special interest the initial explanation made to Agrippa and the company by the governor: " I found that he had done nothing deserving death." This statement, which is one of many other similar statements, points the way before the assembled company to the outcome which is stated in all clearness at the close of the Apostle's speech.

¹Agrippa said to Paul, " You have permission to speak for yourself." Then Paul stretched out his hand and made his defense:

²" I think myself fortunate that it is before you, King Agrippa, I am to make my defense today against all the accusations of the Jews, ³because you are especially familiar with all customs and controversies of the Jews; therefore I beg you to listen to me patiently.

⁴My manner of life from my youth, spent from the beginning among my own nation and at Jerusalem, is known by all the Jews. ⁵They have known for a long time, if they are willing to testify, that according to the strictest party of our religion I have lived as a Pharisee. ⁶And now I stand here on trial for hope in the promise made by God to our fathers, ⁷to which our twelve tribes hope to attain, as they earnestly worship night and day. And for this hope I am accused by Jews, O king! ⁸Why is it thought incredible by any of you that God raises the dead?

⁹I myself was convinced that I ought to do many things in opposing the name of Jesus of Nazareth. ¹⁰And I did so in Jerusa-

lem; I not only shut up many of the saints in prison, by authority from the chief priests, but when they were put to death I cast my vote against them. ¹¹And I punished them often in all the synagogues and tried to make them blaspheme; and in raging fury against them, I persecuted them even to foreign cities.

¹²Thus I journeyed to Damascus with the authority and commission of the chief priests. ¹³At midday, O king, I saw on the way a light from heaven, brighter than the sun, shining round me and those who journeyed with me. ¹⁴And when we had all fallen to the ground, I heard a voice saying to me in the Hebrew language, ' Saul, Saul, why do you persecute me? It hurts you to kick against the goads.' ¹⁵And I said, ' Who are you, Lord? ' And the Lord said, ' I am Jesus whom you are persecuting. ¹⁶But rise and stand upon your feet; for I have appeared to you for this purpose, to appoint you to serve and bear witness to the things in which you have seen me and to those in which I will appear to you, ¹⁷delivering you from the people and from the Gentiles—to whom I send you ¹⁸to open their eyes, that they may turn from darkness to light and from the power of Satan to God, that they may receive forgiveness of sins and a place among those who are sanctified by faith in me.'

¹⁹Wherefore, O King Agrippa, I was not disobedient to the heavenly vision, ²⁰but declared first to those at Damascus, then at Jerusalem and throughout all the country of Judea, and also to the Gentiles, that they should repent and turn to God and perform deeds worthy of their repentance. ²¹For this reason the Jews seized me in the temple and tried to kill me. ²²To this day I have had the help that comes from God, and so I stand here testifying both to small and great, saying nothing but what the prophets and Moses said would come to pass : ²³that the Christ must suffer, and that, by being the first to rise from the dead, he would proclaim light both to the people and to the Gentiles."

This speech is remarkable in many respects. Its literary form is of course due to the author of Acts. We cannot help noting the distinguishing marks of Luke's authorship. But we must nevertheless assume that he was able to obtain reliable information about Paul's meeting with Agrippa and the details of the meeting, that is, unless one accepts that he was himself an eye-witness and a participant. After all, in 24:23 we are told that Paul was given " some liberty " as prisoner and that his friends were allowed to attend " to his needs." We must not forget that this account is part of the first person plural narrative (20:5) which as has already been stated, points to Luke as being the informant.

For the third time the reader of Acts is given Paul's story. For the third time he is presented with an impressive and permanent record of the vocation and personality of the man who followed Christ's call and gave witness to the gospel like no other. It is doubtless highly interesting to put the three accounts (9:1ff.; 22:1ff.; 26:4ff.) side by side. We shall find differences of detail. There is no word-for-word or detail-for-detail repetition. In each of the three accounts we can see Luke's free style of exposition. We find this elsewhere too. It is a sign that we must not look for historical accuracy in the narrow sense. The purpose of Acts, like that of the gospels, is to give us kerygmatic teaching. But it is obvious that the historian's art plays a great part in this. If we study the speech before Agrippa sufficiently slowly and carefully we shall find there many echoes from Paul's letters. We might take as an example the deeply impressive admission of the Apostle in the letter to the Galatians (1:13–24).

If we come to consider individual points in the Apostle's speech, we think first of all of his insistence that he is a Jew. He makes a point of speaking about his " manner of life " among his " own nation." He says of himself that " according

to the strictest party of our religion I have lived as a Pharisee."
And again, as in his speech to the chief priests and the council
(23:6) he confesses to "hope in the promise made by God
to our fathers." Thus he knows himself, like King Agrippa,
to be linked to the "twelve tribes" and their expectation of
the fullness of salvation. He is addressing himself to the longing and hope that was alive and present among many of the
Jews, Pharisees and Essenes. As regards the latter, the scrolls
found in the caves at Qumran witness amply to their hopes
and aspirations. That they prayed literally "night and day"
for the coming of the kingdom can be seen from the daily
timetable of the community at Qumran. We can also find a
pointer to it in Luke 2:37 where he says of the prophetess
Anna that she "did not depart from the temple, worshiping
with fasting and prayer night and day."

Could Paul really invoke on his own behalf the expectation
of the Jews? Was he really able to say: "For this hope I am
accused by Jews, O king"? Or must we assume that Luke,
in the construction of the speech, was unaware of the difference
between the Jewish and the Christian expectation of the last
things? In that case we should be contradicting other statements on salvation in Luke's writings. Luke knew that Israel's
hope was fulfilled in Christ Jesus and that Christ's church, by
reason of this fulfillment, saw the final consummation with
different eyes and different hopes. Paul was able to take over
the Jewish idea of salvation, but in the new sense that had been
made possible for him by Christ's revelation. Thus he is also
thinking of Christ's resurrection when he puts the question:
"Why is it thought incredible by any of you that God raises
the dead?"

That he now regards the Jewish faith in the light of the
Christian belief in salvation is clearly seen when he admits
that in the past he had been convinced he "ought to do many

things in opposing the name of Jesus of Nazareth." And again, as in 22:4ff., he reminds his hearers of the time he so passionately persecuted the church of Jesus. He describes this far more concretely and in far greater detail here than elsewhere, and as a result we get a far clearer and more definite idea of what was said in 8:1ff. and 22:4ff. It is not impossible, as his letters also show, that Paul is speaking in this way here because it is suitable to the occasion. In 1 Cor. 15:9 we read: " I am the least of the apostles, unfit to be called an apostle, because I persecuted the church of God." And in Gal. 1:22f. he writes: " I was still not known by sight to the churches of Christ in Judea; they only heard it said, ' He who once persecuted us is now preaching the faith he once tried to destroy.' "

We can understand that in this description of his past life, Paul is thinking especially of his encounter with Christ at Damascus. This also plays an important part in his speech to the Jewish people (22:6ff.). The account given here is once again evidence of Luke's free style. A slavishly exact repetition of what had been said in 22:6ff. would not be like him. In essentials of course the three accounts (9:1ff.; 22:1ff.; and here) are in agreement. Again we are told of the strange appearance of " light " here even more vividly depicted. And again the conversation between the Lord revealing himself in the light and his persecutor forms the central part of the story: " It hurts you to kick against the goads." This saying is found in one of the plays of Euripides and is also of course a well-known proverb.

Did Luke add it to his account of his own accord? Or had Paul really heard it at the time? It is full of deep meaning. As the animal pulling the cart or the plough feels the sharp stick of his driver if he goes against the driver's will, so too does the man who tries to oppose the will of him who is calling him. This is hardly to say that Paul had already heard the Lord's call before Damascus, but had earlier rejected it. The call refers, after all, to the task laid on Paul from the time of Damascus, which from then on he would no longer be able to escape. From that hour he had been enlisted in a service which would not cease till his death.

Following on his call he is told of his mission in these impressive words: "I have appeared to you for this purpose, to appoint you to serve and bear witness to the things in which you have seen me and to those in which I will appear to you, delivering you from the people and from the Gentiles—to whom I send you." What is meant by this? What did Paul "see"? We read in 1 Cor. 15:8 of the appearances of the Risen Lord who appeared also "last of all" to Paul himself. We note there the close link between that appearance and the other, Easter, appearances. All who carefully read Paul's letters are aware that he feels himself appointed "to serve and bear witness" to the Risen Lord. His sole task is to bear witness to the Resurrection as "servant of Jesus Christ, called to be an apostle, set apart for the gospel of God" (Rom. 1:1). The Risen Lord will never leave him, but will show himself to him again and again in that mysterious communion of which Paul's letters most movingly bear evidence.

Paul knows himself secure in Christ who called him. Thus it is very moving when he, the prisoner of King Agrippa, bears witness to the promise of the Lord to deliver him "from the people and from the Gentiles" to whom he had sent him. The purpose of Acts up to now has been to witness to the Lord's nearness and his protection. And if the words of the imprisoned Apostle witness to it also, this is to express confidence in his future destiny, in accordance with the permanent intention of Acts.

We seem to hear echoes of Old Testament prophetic writings, especially the book of Isaiah, in Paul's description of the task to which he had been called. The " servant " in Is. 42:7 is " to open the eyes that are blind, to bring out the prisoners from the dungeon, from the prison those who sit in darkness." We are reminded how, in Luke 4:17ff., similar words by the prophet Isaiah (61:1ff.) are used to mark the mission of Jesus. The real meaning of the gospel message is put in another way when Paul repeats Jesus' command to him to bring men " from the power of Satan to God," that they may " receive forgiveness of sins and a place among those who are sanctified in me." These words are a genuine expression of the Pauline understanding of salvation. All who know Paul's letters, especially the letter to the Romans, will be able to recognize this.

A " heavenly vision " was the cause of Paul's conversion to witness and preacher of the gospel. We remember passages in his letters where he emphasizes in the strongest possible terms the divine origin of his calling: Gal. 1:1 describes the root and source of his service to the gospel in these words: " Paul an apostle—not from men nor through man, but through Jesus Christ and God the Father, who raised him from the dead." Paul knows himself to be under the direction of God, and he has followed his true path in obedience to this direction, as he assures King Agrippa most solemnly. Damascus stood at the beginning of this path; Jerusalem and the world at large, through which he has been traveling, came afterwards. Even though he was no longer active as a missionary in Jerusalem, Acts nevertheless feels it important to name this town, just as, according to 1:8, th ewitness of the apostles as a whole is recorded as having begun there. Paul is aware of the importance of Jerusalem for his missionary work. We see this in the letter to the Romans (15:19): " From Jerusalem and as far round as Illyricum I have fully preached the gospel of Christ."

And again, as in previous interrogations, Paul points to the hatred of the Jews and their intention to kill him. The reason for their hostility is shown more clearly than before to lie in their religious opposition to him. Yet he does not consider his message to be in contradiction to the Jewish belief in salvation, rightly understood, as this is taught by Moses and the prophets. In Christ the promise given to the people has been fulfilled—in his suffering and above all in his resurrection. We note that it is the resurrection in particular which is mentioned at the end of the speech as the basic and decisive fact of salvation. For Paul it is the light-bearing message of salvation both to Jews and to Gentiles.

We may ask ourselves why Luke depicts Paul as speaking so solemnly and emphatically here about his call and his mission. It cannot be denied of course that the Apostle's words are suitable to the situation as described. Thus he had every reason to speak like this before these particular listeners. He had after all to justify his personal activity and at the same time to speak as messenger of the gospel. Over and above this, however, we have to assume that Luke is trying once more to summarize in this last great speech of Paul's the latter's life and work, in order to show the purity and innocence of his motives and actions. It is not possible in such a situation to separate the historicity of the account from the theological intention.

THE IMPRESSION HIS WORDS MAKE ON AGRIPPA (26:24–32)

[24]*And as he thus made his defense, Festus said with a loud voice, " Paul, you are mad; your great learning is turning you mad."* [25]*But Paul said, " I am not mad, most excellent Festus, but I am speaking the sober truth.* [26]*For the king knows about these things, and to him I speak freely; for I am persuaded that none*

of these things has escaped his notice, for this was not done in a corner. [27]King Agrippa, do you believe the prophets? I know that you believe." [28]And Agrippa said to Paul, " In a short time you think to make me a Christian!" [29]And Paul said, " Whether short or long, I would to God that not only you but also all who hear me this day might become such as I am—except for these chains."

[30]Then the king rose, and the governor and Bernice and those who were sitting with them; [31]and when they had withdrawn, they said to one another, " This man is doing nothing to deserve death or imprisonment." [32]And Agrippa said to Festus, " This man could have been set free if he had not appealed to Caesar."

It happens several times in Acts that Luke does not allow a speaker to finish what he is saying. It was so with Stephen (7:54ff.), with Peter (10:44), with Paul at Athens (17:22), and in the speech to the " people" (22:22). This time it is the governor who interrupts Paul. How should he, enlightened worldly man that he was, have any understanding for what Paul said about the words of the prophets, the sufferings of the Messiah and the resurrection of the dead? The governor's interruption is not to be taken in the spirit of hostile criticism but rather of the sort of sympathetic irony which every Christian has often enough experienced when he has tried to speak about the faith to a group of liberal-minded people. Men do not hold Christianity and theology, the witness of Scripture and revelation, in high esteem. Festus reminds us of Pilate's skeptical remark at the trial of Jesus: " What is truth?"

Paul does not allow himself to be put off. He calls on the king as witness. The beginnings of Christianity are not hidden in mythical darkness. Peter was already able to say to the Roman centurion Cornelius: " You know . . . the word which was

proclaimed throughout all Judea, beginning from Galilee . . ."
(10 : 37). Paul too takes it for granted that Agrippa will be aware
of the circumstances surrounding the life and death of Jesus.
From the beginning of the Christian church, evidence could be
publicly adduced for it. Belief in Christ's saving mystery does
not contradict the witness of history, however much the inner
ground for belief is independent of historical arguments. " King
Agrippa, do you believe the prophets? " Once again the Apostle
shows by means of these words how deeply rooted the gospel
was in Old Testament revelation. Does Agrippa's reply to the
Apostle represent his true feelings? Or is it the result of embar-
rassment caused by deep emotion, and leading to irony as refuge?
Paul in chains represents a stirring picture to the illustrious
company. He stands like a prophet before the children of this
world and despite his external helplessness he remains the witness
of him who had become the beginning and end of his life.
We are reminded of 2 Tim. 2:9: ". . . the gospel for which I
am suffering and wearing fetters like a criminal. But the word
of God is not fettered."

Luke reports the impression which the Apostle's speech
makes on his listeners with special interest: " This man is doing
nothing to deserve death or imprisonment," they said to one
another, and this is confirmed by King Agrippa's judgment :
" This man could have been set free if he had not appealed to
Caesar." If we put this statement alongside all the others which
have been made by the Roman authorities about Paul's position
vis-à-vis the Roman law, it becomes evident that we have here
a climax in the series of witnesses. And again we are forced to
ask whether the statements of these witnesses were written down
in Acts while Paul was still a prisoner and in need of such
statements, or whether, as the majority now hold, they were
recorded long after he was dead.

Paul Is Taken to Rome (27:1—28:31)

They Go from Caesarea to Malta (27:1-28:10)

FIRST PART OF THE JOURNEY TO CRETE (27:1-8)

¹And when it was decided that we should sail for Italy, they delivered Paul and some other prisoners to a centurion of the Augustan cohort, named Julius. ²And embarking in a ship of Adramyttium, which was about to sail to the ports along the coast of Asia, we put to sea, accompanied by Aristarchus, a Macedonian from Thessalonica. ³The next day we put in at Sidon; and Julius treated Paul kindly; and gave him leave to go to his friends and be cared for. ⁴And putting to sea from there we sailed under the lee of Cyprus, because the winds were against us. ⁵And when we had sailed across the sea which is off Cilicia and Pamphylia, we came to Myra in Lycia. ⁶There the centurion found a ship of Alexandria sailing for Italy, and put us on board. ⁷We sailed slowly for a number of days, and arrived with difficulty off Cnidus, and as the wind did not allow us to go on, we sailed under the lee of Crete off Salmone. ⁸Coasting along it with difficulty, we came to a place called Fair Havens, near which was the city of Lasea.

This account of the voyage to Rome and the details that follow have been widely studied by those interested in the navigational problems of ancient times. We are given a great deal of factual information and the writer is clearly an experienced seafaring man. From the precise details given we assume him to have been an eye-witness of the events, and his story to belong to the first person plural account that began with 20:5. Thus it can be traced back to Luke himself. The reader interested in history will note the numerous details about the external aspects of the voyage. But the account is also full of valuable thoughts and insights for the reader who is chiefly concerned with the spiritual content.

A Roman centurion, Julius by name, is in charge of the transportation of the prisoners, of whom Paul is one. Julius treats Paul with every consideration and sign of friendship, and thus acts like all the other Roman officials we have so far encountered who—in contrast to the hostile Jews—behave courteously towards Paul. The Macedonian named Aristarchus, who has been Paul's companion since 20:4, shares with the unnamed Luke, whom we know from the use of the first person plural to be also present, the care of Paul. The names of both these men occur in the letter to the Colossians which was presumably written while Paul was a prisoner at Rome. In Col. 4:10 we read : "Aristarchus my fellow prisoner greets you." And in Col. 4:14 there is mention of "Luke the beloved physician."

Storm at Sea (27:9–26)

⁹*As much time had been lost, and the voyage was already dangerous because the fast had already gone by, Paul advised them, *¹⁰*saying, " Sirs, I perceive that the voyage will be with injury and much loss, not only of the cargo and the ship, but also of our lives." *¹¹*But the centurion paid more attention to the captain and to the owner of the ship than to what Paul said.*

¹²*And because the harbor was not suitable to winter in, the majority advised to put to sea from there, on the chance that somehow they could reach Phoenix, a harbor of Crete, looking northeast and southeast, and winter there.*

¹³*And when the south wind blew gently, supposing that they had obtained their purpose, they weighed anchor and sailed along Crete, close inshore. *¹⁴*But soon a tempestuous wind, called the*

northeaster, struck down from the land; [15]*and when the ship was caught and could not face the wind, we gave way to it and were driven.* [16]*And running under the lee of a small island called Cauda, we managed with difficulty to secure the boat;* [17]*after hoisting it up, they took measures to undergird the ship; then, fearing that they should run on the Syrtis, they lowered the gear, and so were driven.* [18]*As we were violently storm-tossed, they began next day to throw the cargo overboard;* [19]*and the third day they cast out with their own hands the tackle of the ship.* [20]*And when neither sun nor stars appeared for many a day, and no small tempest lay on us, all hope of our being saved was at last abandoned.*

[21]*As they had been long without food, Paul then came forward among them and said, " Men, you should have listened to me, and should not have set sail from Crete and incurred this injury and loss.* [22]*I now bid you take heart; for there will be no loss of life among you, but only of the ship.* [23]*For this very night there stood by me an angel of the God to whom I belong and whom I worship,* [24]*and he said, ' Do not be afraid, Paul; you must stand before Caesar; and lo, God has granted you all those who sail with you.'* [25]*So take heart, men, for I have faith in God that it will be exactly as I have been told.* [26]*But we shall have to run on some island."*

In the detailed description of this memorable voyage we can see the experience of a man who is at home with the sea and ships. But the story also depicts the attentive friend of the Apostle, and the Christian believing in God's nearness. The Apostle's warning that past experience showed the unwisdom of continuing the voyage so late in the year is proof not only that he himself was experienced in these matters, but also that he felt himself responsible for the others and was highly regarded by them, despite being a prisoner. He continues to take a wise and leading part in the seemingly disastrous events that follow. Advising and admonishing the despairing men on the ship, he gives them support and confidence. And thus he witnesses to the truth of his message and to the reality of the God who is protecting him.

The helplessness of those on board is vividly depicted. They try to save their storm-tossed ship by all the means in their power. Their predicament is a striking symbol of the hopelessness of those trying to save their life by purely external means. We think too of the Church at the mercy of storms from within and without, in danger of disintegrating if she relies solely on human strength and human endeavors and is no longer aware that she is always in need of the Lord's presence.

In Paul the Lord is near. Paul is a prisoner, and yet their liberator and rescuer. He presents a touching picture when, in the midst of the raging storm, he moves among the men of the denuded ship, all its tackle and cargo having been thrown overboard, and as witness of the God to whom he " belongs " announces to them their certain rescue. It is a typical sign of the faith that can be seen throughout the whole of Acts and is effective at the very moment when men—and the Church too—are thrown into the most hopeless despair. And again we see how concretely God's power concerns itself with human affairs and brings them to a happy conclusion.

" God has granted you all those who sail with you." We are confronted here by the mystery of the profound relationship existing between man and man. When God shows himself merciful to one man, his mercy is carried over to those who are joined with him in similar circumstances of life. It is irrelevant to ask what might have happened to the men on the ship if Paul had not been with them. Such a question would not lead us to the meaning of the story. We should rejoice in the light-giving truth that a man of grace who is among us will be the occasion of grace for us too. And Paul was a man of grace. It is the special intention of Acts to let this be seen in ever fresh perspective.

SHIPWRECK AND ESCAPE (27:27–44)

[27]*When the fourteenth night had come, as we were drifting across the sea of Adria, about midnight the sailors suspected that they were nearing land.* [28]*So they sounded and found twenty fathoms; a little farther on they sounded again and found fifteen fathoms.* [29]*And fearing that we might run on the rocks, they let out four anchors from the stern, and prayed for day to come.* [30]*And as the sailors were seeking to escape from the ship, and had lowered the boat into the sea, under pretense of laying out anchors from the bow,* [31]*Paul said to the centurion and the soldiers, " Unless these men stay in the ship, you cannot be saved."* [32] *Then the soldiers cut away the ropes of the boat, and let it go.*

[33]*As the day was about to dawn, Paul urged them all to take some food, saying, " Today is the fourteenth day that you have continued in suspense and without food, having taken nothing.* [34]*Therefore I urge you to take some food; it will give you strength since not a hair is to perish from the head of any of you."* [35]*And when he had said this, he took bread, and giving thanks to God in the presence of all he broke it and began to eat.* [36]*Then they·all were encouraged and ate some food themselves.* [37]*(We were in all two hundred and seventy-six persons in the ship.)* [38]*And when they had eaten enough, they lightened the ship, throwing out the wheat into the sea.*

[39]*Now when it was day, they did not recognize the land, but they noticed a bay with a beach, on which they planned if possible to bring the ship ashore.* [40]*So they cast off the anchors and left them in the sea, at the same time loosening the ropes*

that tied the rudders; then hoisting the foresail to the wind they made for the beach. [41]But striking a shoal they ran the vessel aground; the bow stuck and remained immovable, and the stern was broken up by the surf. [42]The soldiers' plan was to kill the prisoners, lest any should swim away and escape; [43]but the centurion, wishing to save Paul, kept them from carrying out their purpose. He ordered those who could swim to throw themselves overboard first and make for the land, [44]and the rest on planks or on pieces of the ship. And so it was that all escaped to land.

To the surprisingly factual description of the nautical circumstances in this passage is linked the interest in the personal destiny of the Apostle and the evidence of the higher power which shows itself effective in and through him. The scene is filled with dramatic tension, the background being the stormy night. That the sailors felt they were nearing land was presumably due to their professional expertise in observing the movement of the waves. Their suspicions were confirmed by means of measurements. They let down anchors and waited tensely for the morning. But Paul the prisoner continued to guide the destiny of the men on board by his words and the power of his personality.

He prevents the sailors from leaving. The soldiers rally to his side. We can only guesss at the tensions and quarrels behind this brief statement. At break of day he goes to the frightened men and with prophetic authority urges them " to take some food." Moved by the spirit of the Lord he says to them : " It will give you strength, since not a hair is to perish from the head of any of you." Paul brings hope and confidence to the whole ship. When all human and earthly efforts prove useless, faith in the power on high provides the only hope.

The words in which Luke describes their meal together have a solemn, even a liturgical sound: " When he had said this, he took bread, and giving thanks to God in the presence of all he broke it and began to eat." It is as though we had been transported into a Jewish household. We forget that Paul is on a storm-tossed ship when, in imitation of the Jewish head of a house, he begins to eat and gives the others a sign to eat also. We are familiar with the solemn description of the breaking of bread from the story of the multiplication of loaves (cf. Lk. 9:16). But this passage obtains its real significance from the breaking of bread with which Jesus gave the Eucharist as his farewell gift to his disciples. Is it Luke's intention in this solemn formulation to indicate that with this breaking of bread Paul was celebrating the Lord's supper? Even if the others on the ship had no understanding of the mystery, they nevertheless would have been deeply impressed by the manner of Paul's eating and would therefore have gained an inner confidence, let alone bodily strength, from their own eating. When Luke gives the number of persons in the ship, this may have been due to his interest, of which we have evidence elsewhere, in statistical details, or does he intend by means of these numbers to point to a mysterious connection with the breaking of bread? We know about the symbolism of numbers in Judaism and its literature. The New Testament knows of it too. But we can no longer interpret the language of numbers.

In the story of the shipwreck, in which we once again notice the writer's strong interest in things nautical, the figure of the Apostle seems to move into the background. And yet everything we read is told because of him. Even though the story describes the rescue of the whole company, it all hangs, as we have seen throughout, on the rescue of the one over whom, at this hour of shipwreck, God is watching. The soldiers want to kill the prisoners, in order to prevent the possibility of their escape. But

Julius, the Roman centurion, puts a stop to their plan. He wanted to " save Paul," says the text in all modesty. We already read in 27 : 3 that he " treated Paul kindly." Thus even in the story of this shipwreck Luke finds the opportunity to point to the kindness of the Roman representative towards Paul. The centurion saved his life. In this account as previously we are able to see the constant effort of Acts to show the Apostle's relationship to the Roman authorities in the best possible light.

They Winter on the Island (28:1–10)

¹After we had escaped, we then learned that the island was called Malta. ²And the natives showed us unusual kindness, for they kindled a fire and welcomed us all, because it had begun to rain and was cold. ³Paul had gathered a bundle of sticks and put them on the fire, when a viper came out because of the heat and fastened on his hand. ⁴When the natives saw the creature hanging from his hand, they said to one another, " No doubt this man is a murderer. Though he has escaped from the sea, justice has not allowed him to live." ⁵He, however, shook off the creature into the fire and suffered no harm. ⁶They waited, expecting him to swell up or suddenly fall down dead; but when they had waited a long time and saw no misfortune come to him, they changed their minds and said that he was a god.

⁷Now in the neighborhood of that place were lands belonging to the chief man of the island, named Publius, who received us and entertained us hospitably for three days. ⁸It happened that the father of Publius lay sick with fever and dysentery; and Paul visited him and prayed, and putting his hands on him healed him. ⁹And when this had taken place, the rest of the people on the island who had diseases also came and were cured. ¹⁰They presented many gifts to us; and when we sailed, they put on board whatever we needed.

It is obvious that this is once again an eye-witness account, for
the first person plural is used. Escaped from the shipwreck,
Paul again experiences God's protective power. In 26:17 the
Lord who had called and sent him told him that he would
deliver him from the people. Malta becomes not only a place
of refuge for the winter, but a dramatic opportunity for Paul
to reveal the power of the Lord's spirit that was active in him.
The viper on his hand, which he fearlessly shook off, became a
sign of the Lord's deliverance. The people of the island, who
knew the viper's poisonous qualities from experience, became
witnesses to this mysterious event. Like the inhabitants of Lystra
who, according to 14:11f., wanted to worship Paul and Barnabas
as gods when they saw the cripple walk, the people of Malta
too believed that Paul could have withstood the bite of the snake
only if he was a god. Are we to laugh at them? Their ideas were
naïve but essentially nearer the truth than the naturalistic concepts of those whose rational way of thinking closes them to all
apprehension of the mysterious.

The Apostle's charismatic gifts are revealed a second time.
The father of their host, Publius, is cured by the prayer of Paul
who put his hands on him. Since Jesus' time healing hands have
been a special mark of his messengers and witnesses. "You shall
receive power when the Holy Spirit has come upon you " (1:8),
said the Risen Lord. Acts witnesses to this " power " in its
descriptions of these extraordinary miracles of healing.

The cures in Malta are the last cures related in Acts. But the
charismatic gift of healing belongs to the permanent treasure
of the Church. In the light of the cures at Malta we need to ask
yet again whether the Church should not pray anew for this gift
of the Holy Spirit (1 Cor. 12:9). The people of Malta who in
their gratitude overwhelm Paul and his companions with honors
and gifts, are an indication of the way men can be influenced by
those who, in preaching the gospel, also care for their bodily

needs and material well-being and use the powers of healing
granted them by the Holy Spirit to the uttermost.

From Malta to Rome (28:11–31)

THEY FIND BRETHREN WHO GREET THEM AND ACCOMPANY THEM (28:11–15)

*11After three months we set sail in a ship which had wintered
in the island, a ship of Alexandria, with the Twin Brothers as
figurehead. 12Putting in at Syracuse, we stayed there for three
days. 13And from there we made a circuit and arrived at
Rhegium; and after one day a south wind sprang up, and on
the second day we came to Puteoli. 14There we found brethren,
and were invited to stay with them for seven days. And so we
came to Rome. 15And the brethren there, when they heard of us,
came as far as the Forum of Appius and Three Taverns to meet
us. On seeing them Paul thanked God and took courage.*

Again we note the nautical interests of our informant, and his
personal recollections of the event. On the bow of the ship he
saw as figurehead the twin patrons of the mariners of ancient
times, Castor and Pollux. Behind this image of the religion of
that time stood the prisoner, Paul. He brings with him the
message which will free men from their dark beliefs and
anxieties and lead them onto the path of true salvation.

In Puteoli (the Pozzuoli of today) the voyage comes to an end.
At that time this town was the harbor of Rome. Thanks to the
good will of the officers accompanying him, Paul was able to
stay a full week with the Christians there. How did that church
arise? It was presumably founded at the same time as the church
at Rome. We have already referred to the Roman church which

was established at an early stage. The letter to the Romans is full of praise of its high repute and the good example it set.

Paul moves on to Rome overland. It was around the year 61, as we calculate the date now. Was Paul the first Apostle to traverse that route? Or had he been preceded by another, by Peter? In our comment on Acts 12:17 we showed that this possibility could not be absolutely excluded. It is true that date and occasion cannot be quoted. But perhaps 12:17 gives a deliberately obscure hint. The Christians at Rome were informed of Paul's arrival from Puteoli. Friends and acquaintances awaited him there. We think of the men and women whom Paul greets so gratefully and respectfully in Rom. 16. We know of course that there are reasons for doubting the place of this chapter in the original letter to the Romans. The great reputation of the Apostle in the Roman church is witnessed to by the fact that members of this church come to meet him from Rome.

"On seeing them Paul thanked God and took courage." What are we to think of this sentence? Even a Paul needs the encouragement of loyal, like-thinking men. It is true, as we have been so vividly shown, that he had been able to offer comfort and support to fearful, hopeless men during storm and shipwreck. But he too was human and had to suffer inwardly and outwardly. His letters are proof of this. It would be good to study these letters not only from the theological point of view but also in the light of the feelings and expressions of sorrow and joy, discouragement and hope, of a sensitive human being.

Paul had been imprisoned in Caesarea for more than two years. He had just experienced a terrible sea voyage. Now he is on his way to Rome—the way he longed to go, as he tells us in Rom. 1:11, and which he now goes as prisoner. We can understand how the encounter with the "brethren" moved him deeply and gave him new confidence. All of us depend, in the troubles of life, on our true friends, on the "brother" or

" sister " who accompanies us on our lonely and forsaken way. When man cares about his fellows in true community, the message of the kingdom of God becomes truly present. Luke had good reason to name the two places where the Roman Christians awaited Paul—the Forum of Appius and the Three Taverns. The two names remind us vividly of the historical reality of the road from Puteoli to Rome. For the Roman readers of Acts these familiar names must have had special overtones.

PAUL MEETS THE LEADERS OF THE JEWS (28:16–29)

[16]*And when we came into Rome, Paul was allowed to stay by himself, with the soldier that guarded him.*

[17]*After three days he called together the local leaders of the Jews; and when they had gathered, he said to them, " Brethren, though I had done nothing against the people or the customs of our fathers, yet I was delivered prisoner from Jerusalem into the hands of the Romans.* [18]*When they had examined me, they wished to set me at liberty, because there was no reason for the death penalty in my case.* [19]*But when the Jews objected, I was compelled to appeal to Caesar—though I had no charge to bring against my nation.* [20]*For this reason therefore I have asked to see you and speak with you, since it is because of the hope of Israel that I am bound with this chain."* [21]*And they said to him, " We have received no letters from Judea about you, and none of the brethren coming here has reported or spoken any evil about you.* [22]*But we desire to hear from you what your views are; for with regard to this sect we know that everywhere it is spoken against."*

[23]*When they had appointed a day for him, they came to him at his lodging in great numbers. And he expounded the matter to them from morning till evening, testifying to the kingdom of*

*God and trying to convince them about Jesus both from the law
of Moses and from the prophets. ²⁴And some were convinced by
what he said, while others disbelieved. ²⁵So, as they disagreed
among themselves, they departed, after Paul had made one
statement: " The Holy Spirit was right in saying to your fathers
through Isaiah the prophet:*

*²⁶Go to this people and say,
You shall indeed hear but never understand,
and you shall indeed see but never perceive.
²⁷For this people's heart has grown dull,
and their ears are heavy of hearing,
and their eyes are closed;
lest they should perceive with their eyes,
and hear with their ears,
and understand with their hearts,
and turn for me to heal them."*

*²⁸Let it be known to you then that this salvation of God has
been sent to the Gentiles; they will listen." ²⁹And when he had
said these words, the Jews departed, holding much dispute among
themselves.*

Paul steps on Roman soil a prisoner. He does not have to stay
within prison walls and is allowed to live in his own quarters,
though under the surveillance of a soldier. This too is evidence
of the consideration shown him by the Romans. Who had he to
thank for this courtesy? The favorable report of the centurion
Julius or his friends in the church at Rome? Or perhaps Luke
and Aristarchus? According to 27:2 they were his companions.
And we learn from the letters he wrote in captivity, presumably
the captivity at Rome, that there were other friends who looked
after Paul. In Col. 4:7–14 we get some idea of the vitality of
this church in which Paul took such delight. But we can also
sense his hard and oppressive lot in the closing of this same

letter to the Colossians: "I, Paul, write this greeting with my own hand. Remember my fetters." Paul signs this letter with his chained hand, and is thereby reminded, physically and mentally, of his lot as a prisoner.

We learn in 28:30 that he stayed in his lodgings for two years. It is surprising that Luke relates nothing about this whole period save the meeting he describes here with the leaders of the Jews. And yet this story belongs to what has been the focal point in Acts from the beginning, particularly in the later accounts— Paul vis-à-vis his own people. He wanted to bring his message first of all to them. But everywhere he experienced rejection and persecution, and it was because of the Jews that he was for the third year now in seemingly hopeless captivity for the purpose of interrogation. All these themes converge when he called the leaders of the Jews to him.

The Jews were once again influential in Rome. Soon after the Emperor Claudius' edict against them around the year 50, of which we read in 18:2, the exiled Jews returned, and under Nero they were once more in good standing. Paul could not have been indifferent to the Roman church's attitude towards him. The Jews had an efficient information service and he would have known that the news of their hostility would have reached Rome. If the trial was to be successful, there must be no disturbances or objections from the Jews, as there had been on earlier occasions. Quite apart from this tactical consideration, there would surely also have been missionary reasons for his talk with them. But the account we are given makes it clearer than ever before how difficult was a really fruitful conversation with his own people. Once again the reader is clearly shown where Paul's real difficulties lay.

Paul stands before the Jews a prisoner. They listen to what he has to say. Again, as with other passages of this sort, we should not be faithful to the intention of Acts if we tried to subject every single statement to a comparison with what was said earlier. We know Luke's free style of composition. But the account is correct in essentials. That Paul " was delivered prisoner from Jerusalem into the hands of the Romans " does not completely coincide with what we are told in 21:27ff., but it approximates to the facts in that originally it was through the Jews that the Apostle was taken prisoner by the Romans. We regard the Apostle's statement that the Jews objected when the Romans wished to set him free, in something of the same spirit. What is true is that on account of the Jews, the Romans were unable to grant him freedom so that Paul was forced to appeal to the judgment of Caesar.

Again he affirms his personal allegiance to all that the Jewish religion held holy and dear—here, before the Jewish leaders. And it is his genuine wish to be able to say that he had " done nothing against the people or the customs of our fathers." Even when he said he was compelled to appeal to Caesar, he continues, he wished it to be understood that he had " no charge to bring against " his people. And he insists in the presence of the Jewish leaders, as he had done before the council (23:6) and the governor Felix (24:15): " It is because of the hope of Israel that I am bound with this chain." Again we know what he had in mind. He is reminding them of the Jewish expectation and the fulfillment of their hopes in Jesus Christ. The Apostle is using the language and concepts of the Jewish faith for what he has to say about the gospel.

The answer of the Jewish leaders is very revealing. They have nothing criminal to accuse him of. This statement of the Jews at Rome is surprising in view of the serious charges levelled against the Apostle by Jews from all over the world. They know that " this sect " is everywhere " spoken against." We have no reason to distrust the statement of these Jews. Their opinion will be particularly important for Luke in view of the trial to come.

The Roman Jews will not become Paul's accusers, if one is to judge from the way they are expressing themselves here. Thus our account is opening the way for a favorable outcome of the trial.

At the same time, however, it throws no very positive light on the religious situation of the Jews. They talk with Paul for the whole of one day. He expounds to them the "kingdom of God." He begins with Moses and the prophets, in order to show them Jesus as the culmination of salvation history. We should learn a great deal if we had a detailed description of the day's talk and its disagreements. But we have only to read the gospels, and Paul's letters, to see how hard the infant church, and in particular a man like Paul, had to struggle to bring together Jewish and Christian ideas. It would have been an intensely active day during which the Roman Jews argued with Paul about the validity of the Christian message of salvation.

The argument was inconclusive. Paul had the same experience as in all previous missionary attempts among the Jews. The gospels had already quoted the somber and harsh words of the prophet Isaiah (6:9f.) in regard to Israel's obduracy, in order to make comprehensible the behavior of the Jews towards Jesus and his message. In the same way Acts too has Paul quote these words at the close of its missionary account, in order to make plain the blindness of the Jews, and especially of their leaders. The very profound ideas in which Paul tries to explore the problem in Romans, chapters 9-11, is evidence of the trouble he took to understand the failure of his people in the history of salvation.

In this final speech of Acts the Apostle's words sound like an echo of all the words we have heard up to now: "Let it be known to you then that this salvation of God has been sent to the Gentiles." We have heard these words whenever Paul saw his message shattered by the incomprehension of the synagogue

and was driven despite himself to the non-Jews. We remember
what he said to the Jews in Antioch of Pisidia: " It was necessary that the word of God should be spoken first to you. Since
you thrust it from you, and judge yourselves unworthy of eternal life, behold, we turn to the Gentiles " (13:46). And to the
Jews in Corinth he said: " Your blood be upon your heads. I
am innocent. From now on I will go to the Gentiles " (18:6).
Thus Acts deliberately has Paul close his final speech with a
reiteration about the failure of the mission to the Jews, and a
special mention of the mission to the Gentiles.

He Spends Two Years in Rome (28:30–31)

[30]*And he lived there two whole years at his own expense, and
welcomed all who came to him, [31]preaching the kingdom of
God and teaching about the Lord Jesus Christ quite openly and
unhindered.*

The book closes with surprising and somewhat disappointing
speed. The reader who has been given a detailed and gripping
account of the proceedings against Paul up to that moment is
inevitably confronted by the question how did the trial end? We
know that numerous attempts have been made to try to understand the reason for this abrupt ending. The question of the
origin of Acts is relevant here. It is difficult to understand this
ending if Acts was written, as is now generally held, after the
year 70 and thus after Paul's death. It would be almost impossible
to explain why Luke should have made the trial sound so gripping, and described it in such detail, if the verdict had long since
been reached. And above all, Paul's condemnation would hardly
be explicable, given that Acts depicts the Roman authorities as
of common accord that he was innocent and that the law could
not reach him.

I confess that the reasons given above prompt me to believe that Acts was written before the conclusion of the trial. This is not the place to give my reasons in detail. I realize that the dating of Luke's gospel is closely connected with that of Acts. If we assume—as was done earlier, and not only by church tradition—that Luke wrote his work when Paul had already been waiting in vain " two whole years " for a verdict, then the account of the trial that we have been given would be immediately understandable as an aid to the imperial tribunal in coming to a verdict about the prisoner. But what meaning could such an account have had after the Apostle's death? Would the description of the sympathy of the Roman authorities have any sense when the church had in the meantime experienced the persecution under Nero, let alone that under Domitian?

The last sentence of all is an apt description of Paul looking back on the " two years " during which he experienced the special favor of the Roman authorities. Proof of this favorable attitude is not only that he was able to live in his own lodgings, though under supervision, but that he had free and generous permission to use these lodgings as a missionary center, and this exceeded all previous favors on the part of the Romans. It is significant, and clearly carefully considered, that Luke ends his account with what sounds like a confident appeal to the Roman tribunal: " . . . quite openly and unhindered." How can we understand this if it was written after the Apostle's martyrdom? But if we assume that it was written in the year 63, then it becomes understandable as a recognition of the generosity Paul had experienced so far, and at the same time an expression of the hope that the favor shown up to now will result in a favorable verdict. Everything we are told from 21 : 14 onwards about Paul ultimately serves this intention of Acts.